In the Name of
Sorrow and Hope

In the Name of Sorrow and Hope

Noa Ben Artzi-Pelossof

Schocken Books   New York

All rights reserved under International and Pan-American Copyright
Conventions. Published in the United States by Schocken Books Inc.,
New York. Distributed by Pantheon Books, a division of
Random House, Inc., New York. Originally published in different
form in hardcover in the United States by Alfred A. Knopf, Inc.,
New York, in 1996.

SCHOCKEN and colophon are trademarks of Schocken Books Inc.

Library of Congress Cataloging-in-Publication Data
Ben Artzi-Pelossof, Noa.
In the name of sorrow and hope / Noa Ben Artzi-Pelossof.
p.   cm.
ISBN 0-8052-1084-9
1. Ben Artzi-Pelossof, Noa. 2. Youth—Israel—Biography.
3. Rabin, Yitzhak, 1922- —Family. 4. Rabin family. I. Title.
CT1919.P38B44   1997   956.9405'092—dc21
[B]   96-48430   CIP

Random House Web Address: http//www.randomhouse.com

Printed in the United States of America
First Paperback Edition

2 4 6 8 9 7 5 3 1

To my Saba, with love, Noale.

Contents

In the Name of
Sorrow and Hope

Prologue

A KING, three presidents, an acting prime minister, the Secretary-General of the United Nations . . . one after the other, they walked slowly to the podium. They spoke solemnly, admiringly, about Yitzhak Rabin, the peacemaker, the politician. Their words floated by me. My mind, still numb with shock, was elsewhere. I looked down at the piece of paper in my hand. I folded it and unfolded it. I tried to see the words I had written on it, but I could only see Grandpa's face. Do it well, I kept telling myself. Noa, show him that you are strong.

Suddenly my name was called out. I could no longer pretend it was a nightmare. My sadness was real. I rose, quite unaware that the entire world was watching me. I thought my legs might give way, but they did not. I walked to the podium and stood there alone. To my left, only yards away, lay Grandpa, also alone.

I looked up and saw a sea of faces. I searched for my family to give me strength. I was speaking for myself. But I knew I also spoke for others.

As soon as I began, I felt Grandpa, my Saba, beside me. He is here. Will he hear me?

"Please excuse me for not wanting to talk about peace. I want to talk about my grandfather. . . ."

At first, I managed to hold back my tears. I heard my voice echoing across Mount Herzl. My head was in a thick fog, but the words kept flowing.

"Grandfather, you were the pillar of fire in front of the camp . . ."

But I could feel myself losing control. Three times I almost collapsed. And later, when I saw myself on television, I remembered the moment, the very words, that released my tears.

". . . I imagine angels are accompanying you now, and I ask them to take care of you because you deserve their protection."

I glanced toward my family and saw my pain mirrored in their faces. I took a deep breath. I was praying that he could hear me, that he could see me or at least that he could feel me. I turned toward the coffin, which was covered with the flag of Israel. For a few seconds, it became the center of the world. He just had to hear my last words to him.

"We will love you, Saba, forever."

4

Only when I looked up for the last time did I see that many people were crying with me. But even then I still did not realize the impact of what I had said. I was relieved to reach the end, to have proven to myself that I could speak to him, to have shown him that I was strong. And if I was sobbing, it was because I knew he had heard me.

I spoke to you, Grandpa, and you would have been proud of me. I spoke to you and you heard me. It was our last conversation on earth, and we separated forever.

I rejoined my family in the front row of mourners. My mother, my stepfather and my brother took me in their arms. And I could finally let myself go. "It's all right now," they whispered. "It's over."

I

"Nothing Will Happen to Me, Noale"

WHAT were you doing when you heard the news?

I think Israelis will always remember the Saturday when my grandfather Yitzhak Rabin was killed. I certainly will never forget that terrible day, November 4, 1995.

The night before, I had spent a great evening with friends at a discotheque, dancing, laughing and enjoying myself into the early hours. I had gotten home around five a.m. and, as always, fell asleep as soon as my head hit the pillow. I think I inherited that talent from my grandfather, the ability to sleep at a moment's notice.

Because we were going to a wedding party, my mother, Dalia, woke me up around noon. It was a sunny fall day in Tel Aviv, one of those days that feel more like spring. Light poured through the windows of my parents' home in Herzelia.

"Noa . . . ? Wake up, Noa!"

As usual, I had trouble waking up, and Mom had to call me three times before I finally stirred. In true character, George, our poodle, had eaten a whole cake, which he had snatched from the kitchen sideboard when no one was looking. And as usual, my mother and my stepfather, Avi, went on ahead of us because my brother, Jonathan, his girlfriend, Rana, and I were not ready. We agreed that we would catch up with them at the party.

AT THAT very same moment, in another part of the city, a young man was planning to assassinate my grandfather.

COCHAV-YA'IR, the town where we were heading, is about a half hour's drive from Herzelia and about five minutes from the green line, the border of Israel before the Six-Day War of 1967. Israel is a very small country.

The reception was held in a garden. It brought together a rather odd collection of people, from politicians and senior army officers to jet-setters and show business types. The groups did not really mix; they tended to linger at different ends of the garden. On this occasion, opposites did not attract. However, if there was one topic of conversation everyone had in common that day, it was the rally scheduled to take place that evening at Kings of Israel Square in the heart of Tel Aviv, a rally organized in support of the peace process and against political violence.

Among the guests at the reception was Gidi Gov, actor, singer, a great comedian and a well-known figure in Israel. Jonathan talked enthusiastically about the possibility of meeting Gov, a hero of mythological proportions to him. But the fact that the guests were separated into groups made contact difficult.

Finally, when Gov went to get a drink, Jonathan, who is not known for his shyness, turned to him with a cheeky smile and said:

"You'd never make a politician. You don't even recognize your fans. You've passed by me several times and each time I tried to catch your attention, but you didn't even notice."

The star, drink in hand, smiled coyly, taken by surprise. But he quickly regained his composure and replied with mock seriousness.

"But it's our privilege as artists to ignore you politicians," he said.

The ice was broken.

We bantered on for a while without joining the others. I could see that Jonathan was very happy to have met his "hero." We left around four p.m., parting from Gov with typical Israeli irony, agreeing that we would surely bump into each other that evening.

Of course. Tens of thousands of people were expected to attend the rally, and our chances of meeting up were minimal at best.

The rally was eagerly anticipated, because it was the first such gathering in Tel Aviv. After dozens of protests well organized by the extreme right against the peace process, this was the first public demonstration in support of the policy, and therefore of great importance. It would show that the silent majority was at last ready to get involved, to prove its support for peace by coming to the rally.

We didn't know for certain if Grandpa would be there, although I hoped so. He seemed to be hesitating because of the "image problem." Apparently it was fine for the opposition to demonstrate against the peace process, but a pro-government rally risked being interpreted as propaganda. In truth, it had been organized by two individuals, Schlomo Lahat, a former mayor of Tel Aviv, who was commonly known by his nickname, Chich, and Jean Frydman, a peace activist and a former member of the French Resistance. The slogan of the rally was: "Yes to Peace, No to Violence." Quite simple and clear.

After lunch, my mother called Grandpa, and I was happy to get the news that Saba would be there after all.

I thought it was only fair that after facing such unfair and brutal criticism, after suffering so many personal and vicious attacks, my grandfather would get his reward. At last he would see that there was a vast number of sane Israelis who backed him, who loved him and who, above all, believed in him and his policies. More than anyone, I knew that he deserved all the praise he would be given.

To be "Yitzhak Rabin's granddaughter" had become something of a habit for me, almost a way of life. When I was born, my brother's nursery school teacher heard of my birth on the radio; that was how Jonathan found out he had a sister. The arrival of Rabin's baby granddaughter was considered newsworthy. But beyond Grandpa's high public profile, first as a soldier and then as a politician, for me he was always first and foremost my grandfather. I knew that when I heard him speak that night, few would be able to share the extraordinary joy I would feel. I so loved, I so love, my grandfather that my love is untouchable, deeply personal.

From a very early age, because of difficult family circumstances resulting from a serious injury suffered by my father, Jonathan and I grew up at my grandparents' house in Ramat Aviv. A very special relationship was forged. My grandparents showed us so much love, understanding and patience that the generations seemed to blur. Grandpa was both my father and my grandfather, and he became the main pillar of my existence, the reference point for my life. He belonged to me. I was his only granddaughter, and he was my guide, my mentor, my model.

So, more than a politician, more than the Prime Minister of Israel, it was my Grandpa who was going to talk that night about peace: our peace, his peace, my peace. I wanted him to hear my admiration for him expressed through thousands of other voices. I wanted him to know that everyone loved him almost as much as I did, or at least I hoped everyone did.

After the wedding party, Jonathan went home, while I stopped off to meet some friends in a restaurant. Hanging out in Tel Aviv's cafés, bars and restaurants is the favorite pastime of the young on weekend afternoons. We laughed heartily and talked a lot of nonsense, hardly trying to resolve all the world's problems.

I did not pay attention to the time. I still needed to return home, to meet up with Jonathan and go to the rally. It was important for us to go together, to see the grandfather we shared addressing the rally. There was something special about going together that only the two of us could understand.

I wanted to stop by to see my grandparents. I had not seen them since Jonathan's birthday, a week earlier, because this Saturday we had not had our traditional family lunch. Saba and Savta, my grandmother, had made their own plans, while we had gone to the wedding party. Perhaps I could just give them a quick hug and kiss.

But I was running late. And, weighing the pros and cons, I decided that it was more important to be present at the rally to express collective support for Saba than to rush across Tel Aviv just to say my own personal hello to him.

"Nothing Will Happen to Me, Noale"

When I got home, around six p.m., to change for the demonstration, I bumped into Jonathan. He was on his way out with Rana. We agreed that I would meet them at Rana's place, and from there we would go to the rally together. I threw on some overalls and a T-shirt and kissed Mom goodbye. She had just undergone an operation and unfortunately could not go to the rally. Being in a crowd, even a supportive one, is not the safest way to recover from surgery. So, while she stayed home to watch the rally on television, Jonathan and I went together, and Avi went with friends.

Mom had spoken to Grandpa twice that afternoon, which was nothing unusual. Visitors to Israel are often struck by our addiction to the telephone. There are telephones in most cars, in pockets, in purses, and they ring cheerfully in restaurants without anyone objecting. Our telephone poles look like trees, with thick cables sprouting like branches.

I drove to Rana's house, and the three of us, plus three other friends, set off in two cars. As usual, the radio was blaring loud rock music. I was thrilled to be going to the rally. I was in a car with Jonathan, and I was not paying much attention to what he was saying. He said something about feeling odd, uneasy, edgy. Something was up. But here we were on our way to the rally, listening to good music: what could go wrong? As Jonathan is often a bit moody, I ignored him.

We arrived in the center of Tel Aviv around seven-thirty and parked some way from the square, behind the Tel Aviv Medical Center. Little did we know that we would be returning to this hospital only a few hours later.

Thousands of people were converging on the square. It was a mild evening, even though it was November. We cut through a public garden. As we walked across the grass, we were all laughing at silly jokes. Jonathan seemed to have forgotten his odd feeling.

We entered Eben-Gavirol Street, the main road leading to the square. It was difficult not to notice the commotion. Buses were bringing people from all over the country and the mood was friendly. There were young and old, couples with babies on their shoulders and teenagers determined not to miss the happening. As we were walking along, a group of kids wearing stickers that said "With Rabin Toward Peace" and "Labor Youth" walked in front of us. Their clothes were literally covered with these badges and stickers. They were there alone, without their parents, so they smoked brazenly. They could not have been more than twelve years old, and this strange mixture of childish provocation and interest in politics made us all laugh. We decided that we must be getting old.

Suddenly we recognized a familiar face. It was none other than Gidi Gov.

"You again?" he said with surprise. "Wow, I really missed you. I'm glad you came. I haven't seen you for so long."

After a short chat, we went our separate ways, walking with the crowds toward the square. We wanted to be as close as possible to the podium. As we advanced, the temperature seemed to rise. I have to admit that there was something pleasant about this heat. It was not suffocating and crushing, like at a rock concert. It seemed more civilized. In their eagerness to express their opposition to violence, people were behaving accordingly.

At eight-twenty, Shimon Peres began to speak, and I knew it would not be long before we heard the voice we were waiting for. Now it was Saba's turn. The crowd grew even more excited. I cannot express the deep feeling of happiness that filled me when I heard the people chanting in rhythm, "Rabin, Rabin."

At the very first words from my grandfather, I began jumping up to try to catch a glimpse of him. But it was impossible. Banners, placards and people far taller than I blocked my view of the distant podium. All my efforts were to no avail. Jonathan, noticing my desperate attempts to see Saba, without a word just lifted me up.

Finally, I saw my grandfather. For a few seconds, I could see the redness of his face under the bright lights, but I could not make out his features. This was the last time I saw my grandfather alive.

I did not know that the countdown had begun and that my world was about to fall apart.

Jonathan put me back on the ground. All the time, Grandpa's voice echoed across the square, interrupted by enthusiastic and prolonged applause and cries of support. He spoke clearly, with a warm voice, but I had heard this same voice so often before that I almost felt I knew what he would say. I no longer needed to see him. It was enough for me, surrounded on all sides by the crowd, to see people's faces, their arms raised high, as they listened with enthusiasm to his speech.

"Violence is undermining the foundations of Israel's democracy. It must be condemned. . . ."

His voice said everything. I was very excited, moved, proud. My stomach was in knots. Bits of his speech, odd phrases, rebounded between the loudspeakers surrounding the square. A large white banner still blocked our view of the podium, but we did not mind. We could feel peace in the air.

". . . Peace is not just a prayer. It is first of all a prayer, but it is also a realistic aspiration of the Jewish people. But peace has enemies who are trying to stand in our way. . . . This rally must broadcast to the people of Israel and the Jewish people around the world and to many in the West and elsewhere, that the people of Israel want peace and support peace. I always believed that most of the people want peace and are ready to take a risk for it."

He did not talk about politics, or the negotiations, or the forthcoming elections. Jonathan and I noticed this immediately. It was difficult to understand why he did not use this stage, this support, to bolster his political position. Thinking about it now, it is as if he knew he would play no role in the next elections, that he understood how the sickness of violence was eating away dangerously at Israeli society. But since we were hardly objective, we interpreted his speech as proof of his greatness. He was reminding people that peace was far more important than any election. To us he seemed the greatest of men.

When he finished his speech, we clapped enthusiastically. We could not help thinking of him as a king, as if he had just been crowned at this event. And now he was being acclaimed by the warm and loving response of the crowd. He felt support coming from all sides.

Knowing him, I also imagine he felt a little uncomfortable. He was a discreet man, timid in many ways. He disliked parades and ceremony. It was rare for him to appear at public meetings of this size. Yet that night, after the speeches were over, he had stood beside Shimon Peres and the well-known singer Miri Aloni to sing the "Song of Peace." It could not have been easy for him, and he probably struggled to stay in tune. He hated singing and dancing. It was the worst form of punishment, he would say.

So often before, I had seen him close up, but on television. This time I had actually been among the crowd.

Later, when I saw the television images of the rally, my eyes blurred by tears, I could almost see his head moving, as if he was trying hard to follow the rhythm and keep in tune. If only I could have sung for him . . .

When the next speaker arrived onstage, we decided to leave. The air in the crowd had become heavy, and it was hard to breathe. We laughed among ourselves: since they had probably counted the crowd already, we could now leave without affecting the statistics for the turnout. I am told there were more than 200,000 people at the rally that night.

We stopped at a kiosk and had a quick drink. The nearby streets were closed to vehicular traffic and thronging with people. It moved me to think that the waves of love rolling toward Rabin were also for my Saba. There is something special about knowing well someone whom other people know only through television and the newspapers. In this case, I felt honored that all these people should love a person who was so very much mine. It may seem odd, but that evening I loved all the people in the square. It is not really in my nature to do so, not typical of my slightly critical, and at times caustic, side. But that evening, all the people seemed wonderful. There was a sort of unbound euphoria, a feeling of victory almost like that on the evening of an election.

There was only one other woman who shared my intense feelings. The woman had been standing beside Saba on the podium, her eyes sparkling, her face lit up with pride. This woman is my grandmother, my Savta, Leah.

We walked to the car, and on the way we bumped into more familiar faces. By a strange coincidence, all of them were friends of my grandparents.

We called Mom to tell her everything had gone off wonderfully well. I must have used the word "wonderful" ten times. And ten times I mentioned Grandpa.

JONATHAN and I returned home alone in separate cars. I was listening to music, but not on the radio, so I did not realize that my grandfather had been shot. It could be that we were laughing and joking at the moment he was gunned down. I say "could" only because I would rather believe that we were not.

Jonathan's car was already in front of the house when I arrived. I parked and was at the front door, about to put my key in the lock, when the front door opened. Jonathan, white as a sheet, was trembling. Avi was standing beside him, pale as well.

"Shhh . . . ," one of them whispered.

I had no idea what was going on. I could faintly hear my mother's voice as she mumbled something into the phone in the living room. I stood frozen at the front door, staring at the two shaking men. Avi was still wearing the sticker from the rally: "Yes to Peace, No to Violence." Then Jonathan, or perhaps it was Avi, said:

"Saba has been shot."

That moment will stay with me for the rest of my life. Instinctively, I asked: "What?"

I had heard what they were saying, but I wanted to make sure it was a mistake.

I said no more. I ran upstairs to put on a sweater, without knowing what I was doing. Thoughts raced through my mind at hysterical speed.

It can't be . . . it didn't happen . . . no, nothing happened to him . . . he was just hurt in the leg . . . we're just going to have a long night . . . we're all going to sit by his bed . . . he'll smile . . . it didn't happen . . . he's OK.

Mom hung up the phone. She ran upstairs to her room, and as she was tying the laces on her shoes, she released bits of sentences, pieces of information.

"Saba has been shot. . . . Savta called from the Shabak [the G.S.S., or Security Service]. . . . She was told it was a blank bullet . . . she doesn't believe it . . . we're on our way there. . . . Saba is not there . . . we don't know where he is."

In a few seconds, the four of us were in the car. We did not exchange a single word. Avi was driving at high speed, ignoring red lights. Mom and Jonathan were sobbing. I was trying to convince myself that what we had heard was simply not true. My teeth were chattering uncontrollably. I could not cry. Often I find it hard to cry. My tears tend to come when I am nervous, not when I am in pain. This is what happened in the car. I was just shaking all over and thinking: It didn't happen, it didn't happen.

"Nothing Will Happen to Me, Noale"

I saw nothing out of the windows except the night and a succession of traffic lights. I found myself turning to God, begging him that Saba would be OK. We arrived at the Shabak. Someone told us that Grandma had already left for the hospital. (We later found out that Grandpa had been taken directly to the hospital from the square as soon as he was shot. Confusion had arisen because his driver, in his eagerness to get to the hospital, had not answered the mobile phone in the car.) Avi turned around quickly and we headed off for the medical center. We switched on the radio and heard the announcement:

"Prime Minister Yitzhak Rabin has been shot tonight."

The radio was quickly switched off, and sobs again replaced the silence. Again, not mine.

By the time we arrived at the hospital, thousands of people had already gathered outside. Jonathan got out to tell the security guards at the gates who we were, to ask them to let us through. When the car door opened, someone recognized Mom, and for a brief moment, while the door was ajar and Jonathan was outside, a photographer stuck his camera inside the car and took a close-up photograph of me. This angered and hurt me. I had grown accustomed to a certain voyeurism because of Grandpa's fame, but was it really necessary now? There was something about taking a photograph of me at that moment that was inhuman, that bordered on evil.

Mom and I ran toward the hospital, while Avi and Jonathan parked the car. We had been told that Grandpa was in the intensive care unit in the basement, and we rushed into the building to take the elevator. In front of the elevator there was a security guard, who would not let us pass. He simply did not know who we were.

"You can't use the elevator," he said. "You have no right to be here."

Mom began arguing with him, pleading with him, then she resigned herself to looking for another door, any door, any way down to Grandpa. For me, it was too much. My nerves were exploding. I felt helpless, desperate. And I kept shouting: "Is there no one here from the G.S.S.? Help us! Tell this guy to let us pass."

The three minutes that went by seemed like an eternity of frustration for us. It was not really the fault of the security guard. He did not recognize us. He was just following instructions. But his obstinacy was like a nightmare. I wanted to strike him. I wanted to shout that my grandfather was down there without us. It was our tragedy, and no one should stop us from joining him. It was my grandfather, for God's sake, mine!

Finally, a G.S.S. agent recognized us and persuaded the guard to let us pass. By then, Jonathan and Avi had joined us, and we all climbed into the elevator and went down a floor.

In the basement, a long corridor led to the operating room. We spotted Grandma from afar in the waiting room, and Mom and Avi rushed up to her. Jonathan and I stayed back, holding on to each other in the corridor, trying to get our breath back, trying to recover our composure so that Savta would not see us in such a state. I remember we crouched down with our backs against the wall, just outside the waiting room, holding hands like frightened children.

Suddenly, in the corridor, a woman, maybe a nurse, passed by in front of us, saying loudly:

"His condition is very serious, but the family does not know yet. . . ."

This unexpected sentence crushed us like a building collapsing on our heads. Just like the photographer outside the hospital, the woman had displayed an unbelievable lack of sensitivity.

After that, it was as if we had entered a long black tunnel. We went into the small waiting room, where Grandma was sitting on one of three beds covered with khaki mattresses. The room was anonymous, soulless, inadequate. It had a tiny Formica-covered table and a steel closet. It had no water, no telephone, no window, no air-conditioning.

Soon the room began filling up with people, mainly Grandpa's political colleagues and friends—President Ezer Weizman; Foreign Minister Shimon Peres; Amnon Shakak, chief of staff of the Israeli Defense Forces; Shimon Sheves, an old and dear family friend; Ethan Haber, Saba's longtime personal aide; the deputy minister of education; the minister of welfare and labor; so many faces coming and going.

The air in the room became stuffy and humid. I overheard a voice:

"He has been hurt by two bullets, one in the spine, one in the chest. . . ."

All around me, I saw eyes shifting in their sockets, like those of scared or wounded animals. Savta was crying with Mom and Jonathan. Jonathan was in a terrible state. He was verging on the hysterical. He had almost lost control. Avi and I tried to calm him down.

There was a brief moment of optimism when the head of the hospital, Professor Gabbi Barabash, joined us in the waiting room, his face white as a sheet. He told us that Grandpa's blood pressure and pulse had stabilized after he was given twenty-one units of blood. Savta asked if that was a good sign. The doctor said it was an improvement, but he was still not out of danger. Savta needed to believe there was still hope, but the doctor was almost like an angel of death for me. I could read on his face that Saba had little chance of making it. I scrutinized his expression, his lips, and found nothing to reassure me.

Ora Namir, the minister of social welfare and labor, kept telling Savta that Saba was a hero. I found no comfort in this idea. Saba had always been my hero, but now was not the time for heroism, not this kind of heroism. I knew that heroism could no longer help him. I could only feel panic, turmoil, despair.

"Nothing Will Happen to Me, Noale"

Savta became really weak; her tears left black stains from her makeup etched on her cheeks. She needed something to drink, but we could find no water. I was afraid something would happen to her. She could not stop crying. She just kept talking to Abale, Daddy in Hebrew, as she had always called her husband. He would call her Sapta, his own special way of pronouncing Savta. In my lifetime, at least, I rarely heard them call each other Leah or Yitzhak. It was always Abale and Sapta, Daddy and Granny.

She talked to him loudly, repeating the same question: "How come they shot you, Abale? Why not me?"

We did not know what to say to her. Perhaps there was nothing to say. There was still no water, no telephone.

It took time for Uncle Yuval to arrive. He had gone to a friend's house from the rally. There, he heard on television that Saba had been shot, but the broadcast showed a woman who said Grandpa was not in any real danger. Uncle Yuval nevertheless followed his instinct and headed to the hospital. Rachel, my grandfather's sister, who lived in a kibbutz in Manara in Upper Galilee, heard the news and immediately began the four-hour drive to Tel Aviv. Uncle Yuval's wife, Eilat, and my cousin Michael also arrived.

Finally, someone connected a telephone line in the room. President Clinton called to give us his support.

I did not want to stay in this crowded room. I did not want to hear the terrible news. I did not want to see Professor Barabash's helpless expression. Above all, I did not want to see Savta's face when she was finally told that Saba was gone.

I stepped into the corridor and sat, as before, on the floor outside the waiting room, hugging my knees, my back against a wall. At the other end of the corridor, just next to the operating room, more people gathered. It seemed to me that the whole of the government had arrived, as well as members of the Knesset and army generals. Nothing seemed to be real—not the place, not the people, not the words. I do not remember what I was thinking about or if I was thinking at all. My grandfather was in danger, I feared he was going to die, but I could understand nothing. I was almost paralyzed by the waiting, the tension, the confusion.

Then came the moment when Shimon Sheves leaned toward me gently and whispered: "Noa, he has passed away."

At that moment, I finally cracked. I had known that the news would come, but I had so desperately hoped I would not hear it. It was only then that I cried, for the first time that evening. Usually sobbing is a release of pain, but this crying was actually painful, not a release. Karin, my stepsister, and David, her boyfriend, arrived. I ran to Karin and we cried in each other's arms.

Someone took out some cigarettes and we all began to smoke, including Avi, who had given up two years earlier. I lit up although I had never smoked before in front

of my grandparents or Avi. I was Noale, the little granddaughter, and little granddaughters do not smoke. But
suddenly I had become nobody's little granddaughter.

We all stood there smoking—Avi, Shlomos Segev, our
family doctor, whose wedding reception we had attended
that afternoon, Yossi Genossar, Saba's adviser and ex-
Shabak member, and other close friends of the family.

Yehezkel Sharabi, one of Saba's regular drivers, a man
who had worked for him for thirty years but was not on
duty that night, sat alone in a corner, sobbing his heart
out. He could not bring himself to talk to Savta that
evening.

Grandma sat crumpled up on one of the beds in the
waiting room.

"I cannot believe I can leave you here and go home
without you, poor Abale," she kept saying.

She did not feel pity for herself. She felt sorry for him,
heartbroken that his life had been cut short. The doctor
hesitated about letting us in to see him. I heard phrases
like "too difficult" and "too tough." We did not give in.
No one moved. We were in a state of shock, not knowing what to do with ourselves. We could not believe that
our hero had really gone. We had to see him just to be
able to try to understand.

Grandma went in first, accompanied by Mom and
Uncle Yuval. Avi, Aunt Eilat and my cousin Michael
followed. Then Jonathan and I entered. The room was
horribly cold.

Grandpa was laid out on a table, covered by some sort of sheet or blanket, I cannot remember which. I could only see his face and his shoulders. Saba's face was still red. It still showed some colors of life. I stepped forward to kiss his face, but the skin was cold. I will never forget that cold, the feeling on my lips. My grandfather, whose skin was always smooth and warm, was lying there lifeless. I will always remember the strange half-smile that was stuck to his lips, frozen on his face, the same special smile that I knew so well. This was the place where I kissed him for the last time, on the left corner of his smile.

We stood there in the icy room, looking at Saba's smile. It was as difficult to leave as it was to stay. Efraim Sneh, the minister of health, entered and leaned over Grandpa's body, sobbing from the depths of his soul. That too is an image that will stay with me forever. I had never before seen an adult crying in this way. So much pain in one evening.

"They" had taken my hero. For me, the assassin was "they." I did not even ask "who?" or "why?" Someone must have told me or I had overheard that a Jew had done it, one of ours. But he, "it," or "they," what did it matter? I was already beyond the world of the assassin. He was the product of a well-oiled system of hatred. He was only a gun; it was unimportant who he was.

My own private world had collapsed. The most important thing was to concentrate on my private loss,

my private pain. It was too early for me to think about
the assassin, to feel hatred, to search for guilt or blame.
Any human attitude toward the assassin seemed to
force comparison between him and Saba. I had no
room for that.

Saba believed in the old saying "All Israel are friends."
He believed this in the same way that he regarded peace
as a form of faith. But now I felt that Saba's faith had
somehow gone wrong. I did not think he needed to pay
the price of peace with his own life. National hero or not,
for me he always was and always would be my hero. And
I wanted my hero alive.

Time after time, he told me: "Nothing will happen to
me, Noale, I promise you."

Later Mom was to say that this was the first time in
her forty-five years that Grandpa had not kept a
promise. But it was someone else who had broken his
promise for him. He was dead.

WE HAD to wait in the basement until the police organized a security escort. Saba's official car was unavailable
because it was drenched in his blood. Waiting there
seemed to prolong the nightmare: We had had enough.
We wanted to leave, but it seemed unthinkable to go
home without him. Savta could not bear to think about
it. She kept saying that they had left their home together
and now she was returning alone.

We left the hospital in a convoy of cars, accompanied by an escort of screaming sirens in a commotion that no longer had any meaning. There was nowhere to rush to.

Outside the hospital, large numbers of people stood in silence, many holding lighted candles, their little flames blinking sadly in the Tel Aviv night. It was the first time that we had had such an escort. Security had never been a concern in our family. And it certainly never worried Grandpa. He never wore a bulletproof vest. He feared nothing. He was a soldier, and he had tamed fear many years earlier.

There was also a crowd outside my grandparents' apartment block. Security became a central issue. Because of the crowd, we had to enter the building through the garbage collection room, a sad and symbolic passage. We entered the house quietly. Savta sat down in an armchair. She could not stop talking to Saba, about Saba. And she kept on asking: "Why you, not me? Why did they do it to you, Abale, poor Abale."

Soon the apartment was full of people, but my mind was in a fog. I can remember little. Who was there? What time was it? Those were irrelevant issues. I was in a daze. Everything had lost its meaning. We wanted to stay together that night. We had already had one separation, the most difficult one, in the hospital. Now we had to stay together. We dared not separate. We were going to sleep at Grandpa's place. Grandma, Mom and I were all held together by pain, desperately trying to fill the void he had left in us.

I was sent to our home in Herzelia to pick up some clothes for myself and my mother. I left Saba's apartment, going past a sea of floating candles, and climbed into a car with Sami, Avi's driver, and a security guard. Me with a security escort? My life had truly changed.

When I reached our house, I found a solitary candle on the garden wall. Someone had put it there for Grandpa. He or she now knew what had happened to him. The whole world knew that Israel's Prime Minister had been murdered.

But did the whole world know that Noa had lost her grandfather?

I called my best friend, Sharon. We could not talk. We just cried. There were no words.

On the way back through Tel Aviv, I again saw large crowds, mourners, tidal waves of tears, but my head was still in a fog.

In the early hours of the morning, everyone had finally left my grandparents' home. We helped Grandma to bed. Still crying and in shock, she kept mumbling snippets of sentences and sighing. Even in that state, she asked for her cleansing water and night cream. It was typical of Grandma not to forget the logical order of things. If Saba had been there, he would certainly have teased her. He liked to say that her meticulousness came from her German background. But he was no longer there, not even for joking.

That night, Mom and I slept in the same bed with Grandma. I have loved that bed since I was tiny because it always seemed so wide. My grandparents and I often used to sleep there together. And there, on that night of mourning, three generations of Saba's women lay together, side by side.

Throughout that night, television showed documentary footage, pictures of Saba at the peace signings, moments from interviews he had given. That night, when young children saw these images, they kept saying to their parents, "Look, Rabin is not dead. He's there! We can see him. Look! He has come back. It's all a lie."

And in silence, as I lay between Savta and Mom, I was saying almost the same thing to my grandfather:

"If you tell me that it is all a sick joke and that you will return, I promise I will blame no one."

11

Earliest Memories

MY GRANDFATHER'S memoirs, which were published in 1979, began like this:

"I make no pretense to be an historian who evaluates events with a measure of so-called objectivity. This book is a personal memoir, and I have depicted events from my own viewpoint, as dictated by the role I played in them."

Today, I have made that statement my own and Grandpa's words comfort me. At the age of nineteen, "total objectivity" and "great historical truths" are overwhelming concepts. My only way of describing my grandfather is through the eyes of a granddaughter, through the deep love, intimate relationship and wide range of feelings that we shared.

I cannot answer all the questions I am asked, nor even those I ask myself. I do not want to address "What if . . . ?" questions. Saba hated that sort of speculation. He always said that one should confront reality as it is and respond to the challenges it offers. I am something of a fatalist and believe in accepting any reality that I cannot control. My attitude toward Grandpa's assassination and the deep loss I feel is identical. This is a reality I have to cope with now, whether I like it or not. "What if?"s are meaningless.

Since his death, my memories of him are distorted by grief. I confuse what he told me as his little Noale with what I read about him in books and newspapers. I find it hard to distinguish what I learned about him before his death from what came after. Memories that flash through my mind remind me of the way he was, the way I knew him so well. Then there are the final images, of the peace rally, the assassination, which fill me with tears and sorrow. Joy and despair are now thrown together, just like on that terrible last Saturday, which began so well and ended so badly.

I would like to assemble in my memory like a precious mosaic all the details of the last moments I spent with him. I usually have good recall, but I passed through the traditional thirty-day mourning period in a state of shock. I could not concentrate. Then, after a while, one very symbolic memory came back to me. With the help of a calendar, I was able to situate it precisely.

We were together on the Saturday before his death.

On the afternoon of October 28, 1995, the family gathered at my grandparents' apartment in Tel Aviv to celebrate Jonathan's twenty-first birthday, which had fallen on the previous day. It was a normal and intimate family lunch. We sat around the dining room table, talking about Israeli politics and discussing what Jonathan would do when his military service ended in December.

Grandpa told us about his trip to New York, just one week earlier, to attend ceremonies marking the fiftieth anniversary of the United Nations. It was a hectic trip, with one official event after another. His schedule was so tight that he had not had time to change clothes between events. He recalled that he even attended one gala dinner in a business suit, when protocol required him to wear a tuxedo. But he preferred to stick to his program of meetings even if that meant looking a bit out of place. That was the way he was, always more interested in substance than in form.

He recounted that, with the dinner about to begin, an aide to President Clinton came to the rescue with a bow tie for him to wear with his business suit. But it was too long, and even though Saba tried to tuck it in, a little "tail" still hung out. So President Clinton himself stepped in to help, borrowing a pair of scissors and cutting off the loose end. We all roared with laughter, and Saba clearly enjoyed telling the story, albeit with some embarrassment. There was something unique about the way he could never overcome his natural shyness and would even blush easily. For all his experience of political life, for all the media attention he received, throughout his life he remained a bit uneasy in public.

Savta liked to tease him about this. She added to Saba's tale by recounting how, during the same United Nations trip, Grandpa walked into a room crowded with the world's statesmen and, rather typically, hung back in a corner, not wanting to impose himself on anyone. After a matter of minutes, his little corner became the center of attention. To any outsider, it was obvious that people would want to meet him, but to Saba it was always a surprise.

After our family lunch, we moved to what we call the "television corner," although it is really part of Saba's office. The room also contains his large library, whose shelves are supposedly organized by subject. Savta was always trying to bring some order to the books. She had little success, but in truth she never stopped trying.

On one of the shelves, I noticed some copies of his 1979 book, *The Rabin Memoirs*. I do not know why it occurred to me precisely at that moment, but I suddenly realized that I did not own a copy of his book. The only copy we had at home had been left in tatters by Jonathan and me when we played with it as children, interested only in the photographs. George, our poodle, then completed the job by chewing the book to pieces, I guess in the pursuit of some intellectual satisfaction.

Saba stretched his arm toward the shelf, grabbed a copy and inscribed it for me:

"To Noale, with love, Saba."

It was exactly one week before his murder. It was the last time I was with him, the last time I could hug and tease him, the last time we were together as a family. And, fatefully, it was then that I had asked for his memoirs.

OUR family is close and has been a source of strength to all of us. We have sometimes joked that we are a bit like a Sicilian Mafia family. We have been tested by crises and as a family have always managed to pull through. Take my birth, for instance. When my mother was pregnant with me, my father, who was a full-time officer in the army and had a promising career ahead of him, was seriously injured in an accident while patrolling the Sinai Desert as part of a military exercise. And in the weeks surrounding my birth, Grandpa was caught in the political cross fire of what became known as the "bank account" scandal. Welcome to the world, Noa. What timing! Yet, despite the turmoil, I never felt deprived of love, attention or understanding.

I was born in Tel Aviv on March 20, 1977, and two weeks later Saba announced his resignation as Prime Minister. What triggered his departure was an old foreign bank account that my grandparents shared when Saba was serving as Israel's ambassador to the United States from 1968 to 1973. The account was actually in Savta's name, since she always looked after financial affairs for the two of them. Saba would never even carry a wallet. He did not need to. He never went shopping and never bought anything. Savta acted as "the bank," as in Monopoly. She managed the account, but it really belonged to both of them. The problem was that when they returned home, the account was not closed. And at the time, Israeli citizens were not allowed to keep bank accounts abroad, even if, as in my grandparents' case, only a few thousand dollars were on deposit.

Years later, when I was studying journalism and communications, we learned in one lesson about news scoops. We were told about the biggest scoop in Israeli history. It was the "Leah Rabin dollar account affair." I cannot pretend that with forty pairs of eyes staring at me I enjoyed studying this case, even if it was supposed to be an intellectual exercise.

Savta had failed to close their account as a result of human error and negligence, but the story soon dominated the media. The Knesset decided not to withdraw Saba's parliamentary immunity. But, instead, Savta would face prosecution. Coming on top of all the other problems faced by the government, the scandal precipitated a political crisis, and Saba decided to resign. He was fifty-five years old, and overnight he went from being a winner to a loser. Suddenly his career looked like just another footnote to Israeli history. He gave up his post as Prime Minister and unswervingly stood by Savta. Even though only Grandma was ordered to appear before a district court and fined, Saba always insisted that he shared responsibility.

With any other diplomat, or with a politician less visible than Grandpa, it would all have been dealt with quietly through the payment of back taxes to the Treasury. But when it involved a Prime Minister in office, the hero of the Six-Day War, a former ambassador to Washington, Yitzhak Rabin no less, a mighty scandal was unavoidable.

His sojourn in the desert had begun. And it was then that he decided to work on his memoirs. It is strange to think that he started to write them at the time of my birth; and that now, at the time of his death, I am writing down my memories of him.

THE situation at home, even without Saba's political troubles, was already difficult enough. My father's accident had left the right side of his body partly paralyzed, and he had also suffered a head injury. Tensions grew between my parents, and Mom decided it would be better if Jonathan and I were spared as much as possible. This is why my brother and I stayed almost exclusively at Saba and Savta's home during the early years of our lives.

I can only hope that my birth brought some consolation to the family during those trying times. I am told that I was an easy baby, who cried little. I was round, weighing close to nine pounds at birth, almost as much as Jonathan. My mother and Grandma were concerned that I was bald until I was eighteen months old. Since I did not have a hair on my head, they did not know how to dress me. They concluded that I would look ridiculous in a dress. So they opted for overalls. Which is probably why to this day I still like wearing overalls.

Mom and Grandma remember me sleeping through the night, which they certainly appreciated. Jonathan, in contrast, was a little devil, who never managed to spend a whole night in his own bed until he was five years old.

Saba was ever present in my childhood. He would never treat me like a child, though, even when I was very young. He did not talk to me in baby language. Rather, when I was only three, he taught me how to play chess. I cannot pretend that I was a genius at the game, but he never lost patience playing with me.

Living in a political family, I was naturally interested in Israel's history and knew about it mainly through Saba's role in it. I considered the parts he played to be the highlights. I learned about Israel's struggle for independence and the Six-Day War in 1967. I began to understand the differences between "opposition party," "majority party" and "government coalition." I can hardly claim it was a full political education, but it was a good beginning.

I think all this led me to have strong opinions, which were very much influenced by Saba and my blind faith in him. During these years, the absence of a real father in my life turned him into a strong "father image" for me. He would take me to kindergarten, tell me stories, go for walks with us. Our ties, often unspoken, were sealed by unconditional love. I had an extra feeling of security when I was around him. He always made me feel that I was the nicest, the wisest and the prettiest little girl in the world. His Noale.

I was his only granddaughter, but he never differentiated between his three grandchildren: he loved us all equally. On my Uncle Yuval's side, there was cousin Michael; on my mother's side, there were Jonathan and I. It was largely because of the circumstances that threw our lives together that Jonathan and I grew closer to Saba.

Funny incidents jump into my memory. On one occasion, when I was about three, Savta had gone to collect Jonathan from a day camp. Saba was left in charge of me, and he told me I could do as I wished but not to be wild. In truth, since he was absorbed in watching tennis on television, he probably would not have noticed if the roof had fallen in. But since he did not want to be disturbed and I particularly wanted to communicate with someone, I went into Savta's dressing room. There, making funny faces in front of the mirror, I communicated with myself. Soon the "dialogue" ran dry, and I fell asleep. And when Savta returned, Saba had no idea where I had gone.

"Are you mad?" she asked Grandpa. "She may have fallen—this is the eighth floor."

"Why would she fall?" he replied, confident I would do nothing that stupid.

Savta was less sure. They looked everywhere for me and eventually found me sound asleep in the dressing room. Everyone was so relieved that no one was angry with me.

Saba never got cross, even when he had every right to do so. One night I was sleeping in his bed while Savta and Mom were traveling abroad. It was winter and we were using an electric blanket. Suddenly, in the early hours of the morning, he sprang out of bed and started shouting:

"Noa, quickly, get up. I have to change the sheets. Quick! Or else we're going to die, the two of us. Quick! Quick!"

Though he must have been convinced that we were both about to be electrocuted, he did not scold me. Once the sheets were changed, he laughed. And until three years ago, when I would sleep at my grandparents' place he would occasionally gently wake me in the middle of the night and jokingly suggest I go to the bathroom.

WHEN I was still small, my mother decided to seek a divorce from my father, a solution she thought best for all of us, particularly Jonathan and me. A divorce under such circumstances is particularly traumatic, and it left everyone wounded. My father suffered and so did we.

As a way of trying to undermine Grandpa's prestige, some Israeli newspapers made an issue of the fact that my mother had decided to leave a man—a soldier—who had been badly injured. But Mom was sure she had done the right thing. And I think her firmness enabled Daddy to recover. Eventually he remarried—his new wife is Esti, and they have four children, Itai, Tamar, Avyatar and Yael—and he has always kept in touch with us over the years.

My mother in turn remarried. Her new husband, Avi, played a central role in our family life, while Karin, his daughter from an earlier marriage, became my new older sister and a close friend. It took a while for Avi and me to grow close, but now we are very good friends and trust each other completely. I almost always consult him about what is going on in my life, from the trivial to the serious. And I know I can always count on him to stand by me.

I think my parents' divorce also drew Jonathan and me into a relationship of intimacy, an alliance that is still strong today. Oddly, though, our closeness contrasts with our very different characters. I hate everything he loves, he loves everything I hate. These differences make for a lot of teasing and fun. And fortunately, we share an identical sense of humor, at times a little caustic or black. In the family, our jokes are known as "lethal."

It is common among young Israelis to say the opposite of what we think, and Jonathan and I do so too. So something "awful" becomes "great," or a journalist who attacked Saba would be praised as "a great man, admirable, wonderful." Sometimes Jonathan and I had our own secret slang or nicknames for people.

We have very different ways of dealing with people. Jonathan is stubborn and talks in a loud voice. He usually gets what he wants by demanding. But I find I can get my way through a quieter, more subtle approach, without my parents even knowing that I have won my point.

More than competing, we complement each other. We grew together almost like twins. We were always surrounded by love, and we shared the same admiration for Saba. When people would ask us about Grandpa, we had set answers that made people feel slightly ridiculous for having asked.

"So what is he like as a grandpa?"

"Like every grandpa."

"Do you ever see him?"

"No . . . he usually wears a paper bag over his head."

"Does he really speak that slowly?"

"No, at home he's a sprinter. . . ."

Naturally, we did not share the intimate details of Grandpa's life at home. Even while writing this book, I feel odd giving away so much.

When he was watching soccer or tennis on television, it was impossible to get him to respond to anything. I could tell him the most amazing stories, I could ask him the most pressing questions, and all he would do was nod distractedly in my direction and say: "Yes, yes."

When I had finished my story or stopped asking questions, he would then turn to me innocently and ask: "What were you saying, Noale?"

It was a family joke: never talk to Grandpa when he is watching soccer or tennis on television.

MY MOTHER is entertained by the comic complicity between her two children. I am of course dedicated to her. She really is the most wonderful woman, objectively speaking. I cannot remember ever having a serious fight with her, although Jonathan would exasperate her at times.

But when we were tiny, she would never get annoyed over little things and certainly not over eating. She would never decide what I could or could not eat, even when my main diet was chocolate. At breakfast at Grandpa's, however, when I would stare miserably at a plate of cereal, Saba would have to keep nudging me.

"Finish up, Noa, come on."

But I never managed to. When he realized that he had not succeeded, he would tell me stories about his own mother.

"You know, when I was young, if I didn't finish up my plate at breakfast, my mother would keep it for lunch and then dinner and then the following day—until I had finished it," he said.

Saba admired his mother enormously. She died of cancer when he was only fifteen. At the time, he was at the Kadouri School, in those days one of the best Jewish boarding schools for agricultural studies. But he managed to arrive at the hospital minutes before she passed away, just in time to say goodbye. Now I know what those minutes meant to him. I arrived too late for my grandfather.

Saba's mother, Rosa Cohen, was an extraordinary woman. She grew up in Russia, one of ten children born into a well-off Russian family. Rosa was not devout and insisted on attending a secular state-run school. Later, through her association with socialist political groups, she became an enthusiastic socialist, so enthusiastic, in fact, that at first it prevented her from becoming a Zionist. As a young woman she could not reconcile her belief in Marx's idea that all traditional nation-states should be abolished with the Zionist call for the creation of a Jewish state.

She supported the idea of the Russian Revolution but soon grew disillusioned with the Bolshevik government. When she came to visit members of her family in Palestine in 1919, she decided to stay. Joining a group of settlers who founded the Kineret kibbutz near Lake Kineret, she was the only woman among about twenty young men. When violence erupted against Jews in

Jerusalem in 1921, she headed for the city, put on a nurse's uniform and began helping the wounded.

Saba's father, Nechemya Rabin, had fled the pogroms of the Ukraine at the age of fifteen and had managed to reach the United States. In 1917 the Allies organized a Jewish Brigade to help liberate Palestine from Turkish occupation and he signed up. Unlike Rosa, he was Zionist from the very beginning.

Saba used to recount how it was thanks to a recruiting officer that his father took the name Rabin. The officer had turned down a volunteer named Rabitzov on the grounds that he had flat feet. So Saba's father promptly went to another recruitment office, where they did not notice his flat feet, and registered himself under a different name. As Nechemya Rabin, he was accepted in the Jewish Brigade. Traveling through Canada, Britain and Egypt, his battalion finally reached Palestine. It was inside the walls of Jerusalem, during the troubles of 1921, that Rosa and Nechemya met. Soon afterward, they were married.

Both held ardent socialist views. Saba, who was born on March 1, 1922, and his younger sister, Rachel, three years his junior, were given a spartan upbringing. They were taught that luxuries were a bad thing and that nothing materialistic beyond the basic necessities of life mattered. Boasting about money and personal achievements was evidence of a weak character. Following the early settlers' pragmatic approach to life, Grandpa was sent to learn practical skills at the agricultural school and was discouraged from wasting his time on intellectual activities.

Rosa remained active in public affairs, although despite her strong political views, she never joined a political party. This was unusual in a country where everything was—and still is in many ways—highly politicized. She was very involved in organizing the Jewish self-defense groups in Haifa and later in Tel Aviv, where they moved in 1923, when Saba was one year old. In Tel Aviv, Rosa also did social work, helping families with problem children, widows who lacked support, and other people in need. Eventually she was elected to the Tel Aviv Municipal Council, where her firm socialism earned her the nickname Red Rosa.

Saba and Savta met in Tel Aviv. Saba was in the Palmach, the secret Zionist fighting force before independence, and by all accounts he was handsome, brave and mysterious—all the traits you would use to describe a hero, all the characteristics that were ascribed to Palmach fighters. Savta was a high school student, the daughter of a wealthy family that had immigrated from Germany. She was pretty, and she still laughs when people look at old photo albums and say, "Leah, we did not know you were so pretty back then."

In the faded black-and-white photographs from that time, Grandma can be seen with long hair flying in the wind, a broad smile across her face, while Saba looks at her timidly. They really looked like movie stars.

Their first meeting has become part of family folklore. As my grandmother often put it: "We met at an ice cream parlor and have been together ever since."

It was 1944, in Tel Aviv. Their friendship began with silent exchanges of glances. They would bump into each other at the ice cream parlor, each inspecting the other from afar, but never saying a word. Finally, Grandma took the first step and went up to Saba, her hand outstretched.

"Hello, my name is Leah, Leah Schlossberg."

From that point on, until November 4, 1995, they were inseparable.

Soon after this first meeting, during World War II, Savta joined a battalion of the Palmach. Her parents' background was very different from that of Saba's. They had left Germany in 1933 and were part of the intellectual and wealthy community of Tel Aviv. They were not surprised to see their twenty-year-old daughter turning into a passionate militant, dedicated to her ideals. Most young women of Grandma's generation, whatever their background, were enthusiastic about playing a role in the struggle to establish the state of Israel.

The deputy commander of her battalion was none other than Yitzhak Rabin, but there was little time for romance. First there was the fight against the British occupation, and Grandpa was arrested and jailed for six months in Gaza. Then, after the United Nations took over the Palestine problem, the Arabs invaded and there was more war. Finally, in the middle of a brief cease-fire during the war of independence, Yitzhak Rabin and Leah Schlossberg were married in Tel Aviv, on August 23, 1948.

Their wedding ceremony is always depicted comically in the family. Both Grandma and Grandpa were nervous, but for very different reasons, which had nothing to do with their marriage vows. Grandma's sense of good taste was deeply offended by her having to wear socks and sandals for the ceremony, whereas Saba was irritated because the rabbi was late. Nothing drove him out of his mind more than unpunctuality. He hated to be late and he hated it when others were late. Having been kept waiting on his wedding day, he vowed, "This is the last time I'm getting married!"

And it was true. Saba and Grandma kept their promise. They were always together. And they still are. Savta said that she had always lived with him and for him. Now, after his death, she continues to live with his memory and in his memory.

Saba always wanted her to be available for their children, to be the ever-present mother that he did not have at home when he was a child. To critics who would accuse him of being too busy to be a proper father to his children, he would reply: "My children have a mother."

Among feminists, he would not be applauded for saying this. But what mattered was that theirs was a true
partnership.

Saba's career was in every way also Savta's career.
There was no "his" or "hers"; everything was "theirs."
Savta may have been *A Full-Time Wife,* as she called
her book, published in 1987, but she was also Saba's
political ally and closest adviser. She had her own independent activities, which included charity work and
Russian language courses. Any doubts about her forti-
tude have been dispelled since Grandpa's death. Not
only has she spoken movingly and with dignity of the
need to carry on his life's work for peace, but she has also
shown a resilience that has surprised many.

I always admired my grandparents' strength, yet it
was always accompanied by warmth, mutual support
and lighthearted banter. They would often stop by our
house in Herzelia after their regular Saturday morning
tennis game. I would always know if Saba had lost
because Grandma would tease him:

"Someone is not happy with his game today."

They made a habit of not playing as a couple in dou-
bles, so Grandpa would invariably reply in the same
tone:

"Yes, my partner let me down."

There was a magnetism between them which I have
rarely, if ever, seen between two people. You did not
need to be part of the family to notice it. Grandpa's

aides got used to hearing their Prime Minister asking "Where's Leah?" if Grandma had disappeared in a crowd. "Where's Leah?" would invariably echo around the room until she was found. It was an endearing call, which brought a knowing smile to the faces of those who became familiar with it.

Friends of mine who visited my grandparents' apartment for the first time were surprised by its welcoming and friendly mood. Its simplicity makes it little different from many others. Apart from the framed photographs of Saba, as well as his Nobel Peace Prize certificate and the security guards at the front door, it would be difficult to believe that someone as prominent as the Prime Minister lived here.

I try to be like my Grandpa, who with a quick wave of his hand would brush aside things that were meaningless or unimportant. But I cannot do that, no matter how much I try. Instead, a passing remark, a tiny incident, a critical comment from a teacher, even the strange look of a friend, can upset me. I do not allow people to see that they have affected me, but I torture myself. I can stay in my room for hours trying to calm myself down.

I think I was helped to overcome my overly sensitive nature by all the fierce criticism that was aimed at Grandpa after he became Prime Minister in 1992. I had to find a way of dealing with it because I felt I had to be able to represent and defend him. I could not allow myself to become furious over every unfair newspaper article, over every attack on Grandpa in the Knesset, over criticism from people who did not know Saba. This forced me to build up a defense mechanism, to seal off my soul from attacks. It enabled me to learn to put both criticism and flattery in perspective.

I think it also helped me to put on a brave front after Saba's death. At the end of the full thirty-day mourning period, I tried to pull myself together, to return to my job in the army, to see friends, to go out. They were not things I felt like doing, but I knew that some routine would help ease my pain and confusion.

I certainly feel older as a result of the assassination. Perhaps I still look like my old self on the outside, but I carry a deep sadness inside me. Often, when I am driving alone, I talk to Grandpa and cry. Yet even though I am crying, just talking to him cheers me up.

I still find it hard to think that life did not stop the moment he was shot. I know that life moves on. I know people lose their dear ones every day. I know that in a way death is a part of our lives. I know all this in my mind. But I cannot accept it. I find it hard to talk about him in the past tense. I find it hard to think of him becoming a memory that fades with time. For me, his presence is still so real. I know that, somewhere, he is watching me grow up without him. I want him to be proud of me. I want to show him I am strong. I want him to be there. That is why I cannot stop asking myself, "How can I possibly live without him?"

III

Growing Up with War

ISRAELI children have always grown up in the shadow of war. From an early age, we are taught that our tiny land is soaked with the blood of soldiers who gave their lives to insure our survival. We learn that we are surrounded by enemies. Therefore our army must be the best. But my generation was fairly lucky. We did not have to face "life-or-death" wars, like those of 1948 or 1973. We grew up in a country with expanded borders and a united Jerusalem as its capital. We even took Zionism for granted. But we too have known war.

The first conflict I remember was the 1982 Lebanon war, although I was only five years old when it began and too young to understand what was happening. The Israeli army had crossed into southern Lebanon in order to neutralize the Palestine Liberation Organization, which kept launching attacks on cities and kibbutzes in northern Israel. But Israeli attacks on the PLO camps of

Sabra and Chatila turned into massacres, and the entire Lebanon operation became a political disaster for the government. Many Israelis were horrified by what had happened in the camps.

I recall being told about a war by my kindergarten teachers and seeing television news bulletins that showed soldiers fighting. Grandpa's sister, Rachel, phoned us with eyewitness accounts of the troop movements across our northern borders. I remember attending my first peace rally, which was organized to protest the Sabra and Chatila massacres. Held in Kings of Israel Square in Tel Aviv, it became known as the "300,000 Peace Rally," since attendance was estimated at this figure. There is nothing unusual in Israel about a five-year-old being taken to a political demonstration. This is how we grow up.

Of course, children everywhere think they are immortal, so war is a game for them. In the school yard, we would often threaten each other with: "Be careful, or my father will come back from the army with his gun. . . ." Whenever we reconstructed battles, we, of course, were the good guys and the Arabs were the bad guys.

At primary school, we were given lessons to familiarize us with the Arab world—their countries, their mentality, their beliefs, their language, their way of life. It must have been difficult for our teachers to handle these topics objectively, because Arabs provoke such emotional reactions, for good or for bad, among Israelis, even children. I was also taught Arabic for five years, but because there was no one to practice with, I could never use the language. So today I remember little of it.

The most important Arab countries for us to learn about were our neighbors, Egypt, Jordan, Syria and Lebanon. We were also taught the difference between Israeli Jews and Israeli Arabs. We were told that Arab women did not have the same rights as Israeli women. In the Arab world, women had a very different role from men in everyday life. Inevitably, we were taught vast generalizations.

But my school had one very concrete program. It would take a busload of kids to Iqsal, an Arab village in Israel, where they would spend the day meeting and playing with Arab children. The Arab children would then pay a return visit to our school and homes. Jonathan had already visited Iqsal, and when it was the Arabs' turn to visit us, I remember that he invited one of the students home for lunch. At the time, such exchanges were considered to be a routine part of school life, and I was hardly taken aback that a young Arab should visit our home.

Then, in December 1987, the Intifada erupted, and my trip to the Arab village was canceled. Instead of getting to know an Arab girl my age, I watched Palestinian youngsters on television insulting and throwing stones at Israeli soldiers. I cannot say that after seeing those violent images I was too keen to meet an Arab girl. It was hard for me, at the age of ten, to form a positive opinion of these people. I found it difficult to understand what they wanted.

THE Intifada, my second "war," was in fact less a war than an uprising by young Palestinians living in the occupied territories. But it had a tremendous impact on Israel and its image in the world. Over the years, Israelis had been brought up with fixed ideas about the Arabs: that they wanted war, that they wanted to drive us into the sea, that they refused to recognize our right to exist. And we were always the ones who wanted peace. Now, suddenly, we were being presented to the world as oppressors who were trampling on the legitimate rights of another people.

At the time, Saba was serving as defense minister in Yitzhak Shamir's coalition government. Grandfathers who are ministers are not in the habit of telling their ten-year-old grandchildren what they do at the office. Likewise, ten-year-old granddaughters do not try to analyze political issues and are expected to trust what adults tell them, especially when they are government ministers. Nevertheless, I had questions, and Saba went to great lengths to answer them and patiently explained Israel's need for a tough response to prevent the uprising from spreading further.

The "war" took place mainly on television, even if it was actually being fought a half hour's drive from our home. The main problem was that television stations throughout the world showed only half the story. It seemed that every night, we would see scenes of Israeli soldiers shooting at and beating young Palestinians. But we never saw the constant provocations, the insults, the ambushes, the buckets of excrement thrown at the soldiers.

Our heavily armed soldiers were portrayed as butchers massacring children who were fighting for freedom. It was a tremendous propaganda victory for the Palestinians. That is why the Intifada set the stage for the future. Most of the world forgot about years of terrorist attacks on Israeli civilians and saw only Israeli soldiers beating "innocent victims." And the PLO showed that it was determined to win recognition of a Palestinian state.

Israel's two main parties, Labor and Likud, were partners in the coalition government, but they disagreed profoundly on how to respond. Labor wanted an international peace conference leading to direct negotiations with the PLO; Likud refused to have any dealings with the "terrorists" of the PLO. As a result, nothing was happening on the peace front.

The meaning of the word *terrorism* was brought home to me when my friend Sharon had a narrow escape. Suddenly terrorism was no longer something that happened only to other people. It now had a face.

Sharon was at the Wailing Wall in Jerusalem, attending a ceremony called Tekes Siyum Tironout, which marked her brother's graduation from basic training in the army. When the ceremony ended and the crowds began to disperse, Sharon and her father climbed into their car, which was parked nearby. They were waiting for Sharon's mother to join them. Her father decided to back up his car slightly so that his wife would be able to spot them more easily. Seconds later, a grenade exploded where the car had been parked. Sharon's father caught sight of one of the terrorists in his rearview mirror, and the man was later identified and arrested. Sharon was in a state of shock for months.

The attack also changed my view of the situation. The constant terrorist attacks and the continuing Intifada made me sense the futility of the way we were living. I knew that Israel's survival was at stake, but I kept thinking that there must be another way. And the more I thought about it, the more I felt that peace was the only solution. Peace seemed impossible, yet it was the only possible escape from the endless cycle of attacks and reprisals.

ON AUGUST 2, 1990, Saddam Hussein ordered Iraq's invasion of Kuwait. This was to be my third "war." When Saddam ran out of reasons to justify his aggression, he called for a new Jihad, or Holy War, against Israel. In his desire to win support in the rest of the Arab world, he sought to link the invasion of Kuwait to the oppression of the Palestinian people by Israel.

It was an absurd argument, enough to make us laugh. But absurd or not, we knew we had to be prepared. The government began distributing gas masks and running spots on television explaining how to use them and how to respond in case of attack. The government also tried to accustom the population to the sound of air-raid sirens. At school, we were warned that a war taking place far away could suddenly arrive on our doorsteps. The greatest fear was that Saddam Hussein might use unconventional weapons, notably missiles carrying poison gas. The consensus was that the best form of protection against chemical warfare was to seal off rooms.

I was fourteen at the time, in eighth grade, my last year of junior high school. I had a carefree life shaped by school, friends and parties. My home environment was happy and secure. I confess that I was not overly alarmed by Iraq's threats. Part of growing up in Israel means becoming aware of potential dangers from an early age. Two or three times a year at school, we would practice going down into the bomb shelter. We were also taught to be on the lookout for suspicious objects in public places that could turn out to be bombs.

I think it is fairly typical of Israelis to respond to wars and violence with a mixture of fatalism, realism, courage and irony. Perhaps because they have seen it all before. On the night of January 14, 1991, just as the U.N.'s ultimatum to Saddam Hussein was about to expire, some people even attended what were called "end of the world" parties.

My attitude to imminent war would certainly have been different if Saba had told me that we should prepare for nuclear war against Saddam Hussein, but he did not. At that moment, he was not in the government, but he had great knowledge of foreign and military affairs, and he believed that Iraq would never attack us with unconventional weapons.

But we had good reason to expect some sort of attack, even though Israel had not joined the coalition forces organized by the United States to free Kuwait. Saddam Hussein had repeatedly warned that Israel would be the first target. And within Israel, Tel Aviv, the country's economic capital, would be the target of choice. If missiles were fired, they would be aimed at the city's government buildings, including the defense ministry. It was understood that people living in Jerusalem and along the borders would be safer.

On January 17, the first Scud missiles fell on Israel, two on Tel Aviv and one on Haifa, wounding twelve people. The following day, CNN informed us that American Patriot antimissile missiles had now been deployed on our territory. But one Scud slipped through these defenses and left three people dead and more than one hundred wounded in Tel Aviv. Later, missiles again struck Tel Aviv and Haifa.

Now the war was real. Schools were closed and people began stocking up huge amounts of food. Everyone was home by six p.m. Going out after that was considered risky.

In the beginning, the main fear was poison gas and not conventional missiles, so we were told to move to the highest rooms of our houses in case of attack, because toxic gas stays close to the ground. Chemical warfare is a cowardly way of fighting, but Saddam Hussein was capable of it. He had shown that in his war with Iran. And for Jews, gas stirred particularly horrible memories.

The first time the siren went off, I was fast asleep at home in Herzelia. Mom woke me up, and following instructions, we put on large and ugly gas masks. We had been trained to use them at school. That night, we went straight to our parents' bedroom and sat there, listening to the radio and watching television. We did not talk much, because it was difficult to make ourselves understood while wearing a mask. It was a bit like being inside an aquarium. We had to wait four hours before the all-clear sounded—four long, nervous hours.

Saba, however, never bothered to use his gas mask. He had even appeared on television, stating his opinion that Iraq would not use poison gas against Israel. The former defense minister's opinion carried weight. Soon we—along with almost everyone else—gave up concentrating in upstairs rooms, which were vulnerable to explosive missiles. Instead, we headed for our underground shelter whenever the siren sounded. George, our dog, was terrified by the noise and was always the first to reach the door of the shelter.

At home, we developed our own routine in response to the air-raid warnings. Even though we no longer felt the threat of chemical warfare, we, unlike Grandpa, continued wearing our gas masks and sealing the shelter. In the end these precautions proved unnecessary, but they reassured us. Jonathan's job was to soak towels in bicarbonate of soda diluted in water and place them on the floor at the bottom of the door. We were told that bicarbonate of soda would neutralize any gas that seeped through. Once everyone was inside, the door was sealed with nylon and masking tape. My job was to turn down the heat in the house.

Our shelter, reachable down a staircase directly from the sitting room, was really a large room. It had a television, radio, telephone, sofa and bed. We would stay there until we heard the all-clear, then we would go back to our upstairs bedrooms.

It may seem ridiculous, but I enjoyed some aspects of the war. We spent a lot of time at home as a family, eating and playing Monopoly and backgammon. But the nights were long, particularly for Avi, who felt responsible for waking us up at the threat of attack. After a while, a "silent" radio station was introduced for the many people who, like Avi, were unable to sleep. You could leave your radio on full volume and it would remain silent, coming alive only to broadcast the sound of the sirens. After the danger had passed, it fell quiet again, allowing people to go back to sleep.

When the war began in January 1991, many residents of Tel Aviv took refuge in Eilat, the popular beach resort at the northern tip of the Gulf of Aqaba. Eilat had been caught up in the Six-Day War. But for Israelis, it had become synonymous with sun, fun and holidays. And now, although American aircraft carriers were stationed not far away in the Red Sea, Eilat was still safer than Tel Aviv.

My parents never dreamed of fleeing Tel Aviv. My grandparents didn't either, even though their apartment, on the top floor of a building, was more vulnerable to attack than most. I think my mother worried more about them than about us. We lived in a house some distance from the city center and its strategic buildings.

One night Mom insisted that Grandpa and Grandma come to sleep at our house in Herzelia. It was not the most exciting invitation they had ever received, but they reluctantly agreed. I thought it was amusing to have them at our place. They were so independent and used to doing what they wanted to at home. Suddenly they were guests. When the siren went off that night, we shouted at them to hurry and come downstairs. But Grandma decided this was a good moment to have a shower, which of course took time and delayed sealing the shelter. I remember that Saba was quite annoyed with her.

"We're not at home," he said. "Here you have to do as the children say!"

How could I really be worried about missiles when Saba was more concerned about how he should behave as a guest?

Protected by the adults who surrounded me, I understood my parents' anguish only after the war was over. One morning during the fighting, Avi and Mom found a piece of a Scud missile in our garden. It had fallen during the previous night's raid, but they decided not to show it to Jonathan and me and instead handed it over to the authorities. Three months later, they finally told us about the incident. I suppose Jonathan and I should have been shaken, but in fact we were sorry not to have seen what it looked like, and did not dwell on how close we had been to the war.

For me, this was a war of novelties, like CNN. At the time, Israel had only one television station, and it was government-controlled. In the weeks before the war broke out, Avi went to great lengths to have a satellite dish installed at our home. He wanted to make sure we knew exactly what was going on. Once the attacks began, CNN became the anchor of our lives. Although all reporting from Israel was subject to military censorship, CNN gave us a broader view of what was happening elsewhere in the region. When it reported that Iraq had launched an attack on Saudi Arabia, we knew that we had thirty minutes in which to get organized, have a shower, take George into the garden, before Israel was attacked. Our calculation never failed. It was just one of the many quirks of that weird war.

ALL my views of these wars were formed without my ever being on the firing line. I never thought Israel was in serious danger, I never felt my own family was at risk. I could not believe that we were going to be killed in a war I could watch on television. It was a war, but for me it was a war without a front line.

Earlier generations grew up with different wars. My wars affected me, but not in the way that outsiders might imagine. Saba taught me that it was important to know how to contain fear and how to respond pragmatically. He fervently believed that you should never allow fear to freeze you, to move you off your planned course, to make you change your habits or beliefs. Saba had survived many wars. He knew how to deal with them. It was peace that killed him.

I tried to follow his example. And most of the time I succeeded. It was only when I was asleep that I would find myself haunted by fears I could laugh off in the daytime. I started dreaming more and more about death. And during "my" wars, these nightmares became more frequent, more sinister. I would dream that I was standing at my mother's funeral. Another night, I would be at

Jonathan's funeral; or at Avi's or Grandma's. I even dreamed of my own funeral.

But what I remember most vividly today is that Grandpa never appeared in these nightmares. Even when fear took hold of my subconscious in the middle of the night, the only loved one whom I never buried, who never had a funeral, who never died, was Saba.

IV

The Hope for Something Different

T HE ONLY war that had a profound effect on my
life, the one that I could never get used to, was neither front-page news nor the breaking story on CNN. It
was Jonathan's war.

When he joined the army in December 1992, I realized that nothing would ever be the same again. Jonathan
had always been my best friend, my big brother, my other
half. Whenever we did something, even if we did it sepa-
rately, it became "ours." But now that he was a soldier, I
recognized that the separation would take on different
proportions.

Jonathan was eighteen and a soldier; I was two and a
half years younger and still a student. For the first time
in our lives, the age difference between us became mean-
ingful. We were living in two different worlds. The
security situation in the country was "normal," yet for all
this "normality," Jonathan would soon be sent to fight
in the streets of the occupied territories or in southern

Lebanon. Israel was not technically at war, but daily life resembled war in the most basic and terrible ways: people were losing their lives.

Anyone who has seen a loved one leave home can understand my sense of loss. Jonathan had always been there. He hated to sleep away. He would spend hours lounging in his bedroom, in the kitchen, in the living room. I always knew where he had last been from the trail of disorder he left behind. Emotionally and physically, his presence at home was deeply felt.

Now his bedroom door was closed. We ate breakfast without him. He was not there to yell at me when I spent too long on the telephone. He no longer messed up my room. I found myself missing all the things about him that used to irritate me. The house seemed empty.

The first time I saw him in uniform, I burst out laughing: the clothes looked quite out of place on him. I could not adjust to the idea that from one day to the next he had become so upright, so grown up. This "soldier" reminded me of the naughty boy whose disarming wit enabled him to go everywhere and get everything. Memories of that rascal came flooding back to me.

I remembered an incident when he was about six and I was three and a half. Grandpa was using a tape recorder to dictate his memoirs, and one morning he could not find it.

"Noa, have you seen my little tape recorder?" Saba asked.

I had seen Jonathan take it from Grandpa's drawer without permission, but I did not say a word, such was the solidarity between us. I could not lie to Grandpa, so I kept my head down; concentrating on my drawing, I remained silent.

Then two days later Jonathan returned the machine to the drawer, and I waited for Grandpa to find it.

"Ah, here's my tape recorder," he said with apparent surprise. "It was right in front of my eyes all the time and I didn't see it. How silly of me!"

I was sure he knew what had happened, because he had looked everywhere for it for two days. But since Jonathan, the "little thief," had returned it, the matter was closed.

Now the "little thief" was a soldier. And Grandpa was deeply proud of him. Without being pressed to do so, Jonathan had volunteered for the paratroop brigade, a very tough combat unit.

In Israel, family and friends always accompany young men and women to the central call-up base on their first day in the army, and we were no different. Jonathan had four months of basic training ahead of him before he would go on to train as a paratrooper and paramedic. He was far from home, but he would call us often; we would send him food parcels of coffee and cereals.

I would write to him regularly to update him on what was going on at home and to tell him how awful it was not to have him around. I would count the days leading up to his home leave, which, although erratic, averaged one weekend every two weeks. Knowing that his trips home could be canceled at the last minute, we celebrated only when we saw him walking through the front door.

From my earliest days, we had spoken about peace. And now Jonathan was at the front.

After his first four months, he was sent to the West Bank and became an eyewitness to the Intifada. He was now part of the "war" being fought against stone-throwing children. He would tell me that he spent his days chasing kids and his nights dreaming that the kids were chasing him. Like many young Israeli men of his generation, he became a player in this historical standoff. His four months there seemed to me to last forever.

But the dangers that he faced on the West Bank were insignificant compared with those that followed. After another stint of training back at base camp, he was sent to the fragile "no-man's-land" between Israel and Lebanon, where anything could happen. I used to scour the newspapers daily, trying to find out everything I could about that front. But for all the information I gathered, I still felt impotent.

I began to have nightmares that he had been killed. Mom had trouble sleeping too. All we could do was tell each other our dreams. It brought us closer, even though I grew nervous and irritable. Sometimes I would visit friends just to take my mind off it. I needed to laugh and to shake off my dark thoughts, but they would return to me every night. Mom would dream that Jonathan was wounded, that he was running and falling, that he needed help, while I kept dreaming that I was attending his funeral.

Despite the discomforts of life in the army, my brother tried to keep up his spirits. I remember his coming home one weekend and telling my mother: "Lebanon is beautiful. . . . It's just like Switzerland, except there's no war in Switzerland."

In southern Lebanon, the war was never far away. One Friday, we learned that one of Jonathan's friends from school had just been killed by a rocket that struck his head. Our entire school attended the funeral on Sunday. It was the first time I had stood by the coffin of a soldier, a soldier who was Jonathan's age, someone who not long ago had been a student like me and now was dead.

Memorial Day is the annual tribute paid to Israeli soldiers who have fallen in wars. This is more of a reminder to the rest of the country than for the bereaving families; the relatives do not need a special day to remind them of their loss. Only now do I know firsthand how painful bereavement can be.

More than ever, I tried to understand what the fighting was about. It helped being able to listen to Grandpa. He had thought a great deal about war and peace, and when we talked, I could see that it occupied his mind. When a soldier was killed, he took it personally. He would frown and go silent. Then he would find out exactly what had happened, at what time, in what place. The death of a soldier meant something had gone wrong. Every death needed to be clarified.

But with his grandson now a soldier, I think Saba began to look at things in a new way. It was as if he himself had become a soldier again. He literally glowed with pride when Jonathan first appeared before him in uniform. He put his hand on Jonathan's shoulder, and with that mysterious half-smile, he nodded knowingly at his grandson's transformation.

But with his admiration came a feeling of dread. Before him stood the fourth generation of the Rabin family to carry a weapon to defend Israel's right to exist. His father, himself, his son, and now his grandson—all had been sent off to fight. His former son-in-law, my father, had also been badly injured while serving in the army. How many more generations of soldiers would be needed before Israel was secure?

I cannot say that Grandpa's desire for peace was awakened by the dangers facing Jonathan, because I believe he always wanted peace. But his resolve was definitely strengthened. And there was another, perhaps more important, difference now. Beginning in June 1992, Saba was again Prime Minister of Israel, and if there came a chance for peace, I was sure he would grab it.

He never expressed fears for Jonathan's life, but he clearly worried about him. One evening when Grandpa was going to dinner at the home of the Egyptian ambassador, Jonathan phoned to say that he urgently needed to talk to him. And even though Saba was obsessive about being punctual and was already running late, he found the time. He answered:

"Fine, I have ten minutes."

On the way to the ambassador's residence, he stopped by our home and sat with Jonathan in the living room. For about half an hour, they discussed strategy and maps and all sorts of military questions that were on Jonathan's mind. It was one of those rare occasions when Grandpa was late for an appointment. He had acknowledged another priority.

As I HAD hoped, from the moment Grandpa returned to office as Prime Minister, he began raising hopes for peace. Nine months earlier, there had been a flurry of optimism when Israel sat down with its traditional Arab enemies at the Middle East peace conference in Madrid, but then the talks had bogged down. Now, in order to break the impasse, Grandpa was ready to show good-will. He promised to "freeze" the construction of new Israeli settlements in the occupied territories, and he began to use the phrase "Palestinian autonomy," as envisaged by the Camp David agreements. He also held out a hand of friendship to the PLO and Jordan and offered to end the conflict with Syria.

The Hope for Something Different

As soon as secret peace negotiations with the PLO began, Saba seemed to change. He was more introspective and pensive, busier than ever. Now I understand why. He was struggling to find a bridge between his deep distrust of the Arabs and his profound desire for peace. When I think about the way I shut myself in my room when I have the smallest problem, I can imagine how much he wrestled with himself before deciding what was best for Israel.

Naturally he did not share the full picture of the behind-the-scenes negotiations with us at home. Instead, we would get inklings as to his thinking, snippets of information. He would also probe us for information. He wanted to know what young people thought, what ideas and worries I and others discussed at school, in cafés, in the streets. After all, it was our future he was preparing. All those speeches we had heard about "building an Israel for future generations" suddenly began to take on real meaning for me.

Sometimes the generation gap was apparent at home. People my age had been raised in an Israel very different from that of our parents and grandparents. We had more freedom and independence, and we had rap music, fashionable clothes and McDonald's to divert us. From an early age, we wandered the streets in groups, staying out long after midnight, talking about everything, enjoying ourselves. We wanted to live in a country at peace. And, for me, if this meant handing back some land, why not?

I had begun to form my own views about the situation, and they were considered to be to the "left" of Grandpa's. Today, the left and right in Israeli politics are defined above all in terms of their respective attitudes toward the peace process. I thought Israel should be more daring in seeking peace with its neighbors. Although I could only distantly remember the war in Lebanon and had been a mere spectator in the Intifada and the Gulf war, I thought a lot about the relationship between land and security. Specifically, it seemed to me that occupying "foreign" lands did not automatically guarantee security. In some cases, I agreed, land was a strategic element, but not in others.

I had an impatient yearning for peace, fueled by Jonathan's military service and my natural youthful optimism. But Grandpa would never talk down to me when I called for miraculous remedies. He would always hear me out first and then temper my idealism with a dose of hard-nosed realism.

Saba's generation was bound to see things differently. It had fought and died to create Israel and unify Jerusalem. Saba personally had been on the front lines of many wars. He was better acquainted with the enemies than I and was therefore more wary.

He knew it was vital for Israel to be strong. He knew that we could not make peace on just any terms. But when peace talks bogged down, he was also capable of saying:

"OK, things are not getting any better, so let's change our approach and try something different. We have dreamed of living in peace on this land for the past two thousand years, so let's try peace."

He could have acted differently. When the negotiations were going nowhere, he could have sat back and thought, Well, we have always won our wars, we can always crush the Palestinians, we are not scared of isolation. We know how to fight and we know how to win.

But Saba had the courage and imagination to believe peace was possible. For him and those his age, it required a profound rethinking of almost everything they had learned and known. Saba changed his mind, and it made me doubly proud of him.

Moves toward peace, though, divided Israel, with the extreme right and the religious parties strongly opposed to it.

The Golan Heights posed a particularly difficult dilemma. Until 1967, Golan served as the launching area for Syrian rockets aimed at Israeli villages and kibbutzes. When the Six-Day War broke out, our troops quickly took the heights and assured the safety of the villages below. But in the Yom Kippur War of October 1973, while Egypt advanced into Sinai, the Syrians attacked our positions on Golan. Our forces held their ground, but only after a furious tank battle.

Now the Golan Heights were again at the center of the peace debate. Syria said that peace with Israel was possible only if all of the Golan Heights was returned, while many Israelis believed that none of the occupied area should be abandoned. My view was that if Syria really wanted peace, it should content itself with only part of the hills overlooking Israel. But was Israel willing to go halfway?

I had lengthy discussions with Grandpa about the Golan Heights, partly because it worried me that his political enemies were accusing him of dishonesty. During the 1992 election campaign, he had said that "we will not go down from the Golan Heights." However, shortly after he arrived in office, he was being portrayed as "the man who will surrender Golan even though he promised not to." This was an accusation that I heard coming not only from the right-wing opposition but from people my own age at school as well. And I did not know how to respond.

One night over dinner, I raised the issue. I mentioned the charges against him and I listened to his reply.

"The party's political platform said that 'there will not be a total withdrawal from the Golan Heights.' My intention, then, is to hand over to Syria not all of the occupied land but only a part of the territory, in exchange for peace."

I understood that this was something of a semantic distinction, but it was a valid one, and it helped me to answer his critics and to address my own concerns.

I asked him if it disturbed him that his own words were used as propaganda against him by the extreme right. He answered in much the same way: that he adhered to the party platform and that nothing was more important than peace.

But he rarely bothered to answer his critics directly. He felt no need to explain his motives because, for him, his actions spoke for themselves.

I always listened to him carefully. He had so much detailed information at his fingertips. For every argument I could come up with, he would give me ten complex counterarguments in return. It was very difficult not to be convinced by his reasoning, which was backed by so much knowledge and experience. He covered every point so exhaustively in his answers that I was often left with no questions to ask.

"Mmm . . . although I must admit I saw it differently before, now that you have explained things . . . you've got a point," I would say.

I took his arguments seriously because I believed him. However, I also considered myself to be his representative, with a duty to be able to defend his point of view to others.

In truth, I think any politician should have understanding in his own house. He has so many negative things thrown at him in the press and in parliament that he needs some peace and support when he returns home. In Saba's case, this came easily. His family was always a safe haven for him.

IN 1994, I remember participating in a live television program with other young people, when we were asked questions about the "land-for-peace" policy. Among the many guests on the show was a young boy from Kiriat Arba who was stubbornly against the peace process. From the way he was dressed, it was obvious he was devoutly religious. But he did not couch his arguments in biblical terms. Instead, he justified his position by saying that peace was only possible when it was sought from a position of strength; that, under any other conditions, peace could be construed only as a sign of weakness. As peace was the reward for the strong, and Israel had not been victorious against the Palestinians, he claimed that the government's peace policy was forcing Israel to bow before its enemies and concede defeat.

This boy was asked by the interviewer if he minded that peace, as he interpreted it, might take several generations to achieve. Did he mind the idea that in years to come, if he were to become a television presenter, he might still be discussing the possibility, and not the reality, of peace? The boy from Kiriat Arba answered,

"Although I hope it will not take generations, we must never give up our home, we must never give up our land."

I remember being particularly impressed by the courage of one participant on the show. He had been five years old when he had lost his father in a PLO attack. Ten years later he was encouraging and defending the negotiations with the Palestinians. He had no hunger for revenge; he did not seek retribution from the Palestinians. Instead, he sought reconciliation, in the hope that lives like his father's could be saved. This, for me, was a sign of real strength.

When it was my turn to speak, I chose my words carefully, knowing that whatever I said might be used against my grandfather. The interviewer spared me any direct confrontation with the "anti-peace lobby," and instead asked me more general questions, like:

"How would you define heroism?"

"Heroism is about taking an action which represents a breakthrough, and then assuming full responsibility for it, even if it's a failure," I answered.

"What does peace mean to you?"

I remember my reply began, "It means not having to worry about the men who patrol the frontiers. . . ."

Had the program taken place six months later, the voices that stood out against the peace process may well have fallen back on religious arguments to undermine it. At the time this program was broadcast, it was still rare, at least on television, to hear people doing so.

But the exponents of these arguments did not remain camera shy for long. Their reasoning closely follows the letter of the Bible. They refer to the holiness of this land which God gave us to care for. They argue that to hand over this land is to violate the kingdom of King David, and therefore to go against God's will. If the land of Israel is intrinsically holy, then safeguarding the frontiers becomes more valuable than safeguarding life.

But for me, it is peace in the land of Israel that is holy. I have little in common with the advocates of "land at any cost" arguments. The majority of these people have received a completely different education from mine. Extreme orthodox religious schools teach their pupils to believe that every word of the Bible must be obeyed. The Bible dictates their every movement. I rarely encounter these students because we live in two separate worlds. We do not dress alike and we do not hang out in the same places. They keep a traditional lifestyle, which is ruled by the Bible, whereas we live a modern, everyday life.

I may be part of a people almost four thousand years old, but I am also nineteen years old and I do not want to go back to the beginning. In our family, we follow certain Jewish traditions, such as fasting during Yom Kippur, but not all of them. I know the Ten Commandments by heart. Grandpa, who was not devout, taught me an additional commandment, one I feel particularly attached to.

"Noa," he said, "always tell the truth."

My position is that you do not have to practice a religion in order to have a religion. Likewise, religions that are different in form need not contradict each other in substance. What people forget is that the Jews and the Muslims have the same God; we call him Elohim and they call him Allah. We also share an important prophet; we call him Abraham and they call him Ibrahim. The main difference is that for us, Moses and the other prophets were human; for them, the prophet Muhammad is holy. So if we have so much in common, why can't Jews and Arabs live together?

Yet after everything the Jews have been through—after the diaspora, the pogroms, the Zionist struggle, the Holocaust, the international isolation, and the wars—we must remain on the alert. We must be vigilant about how Jews are treated around the world. And we must safeguard our democracy.

If I can speak freely, it is because I live in a democracy, but even in Israel it has its enemies. Many on the extreme right see democracy as a convenient vehicle for achieving political power. But I am not convinced they actually believe in democracy. They certainly do not behave as if they do.

In December 1995, barely one month after Saba was killed, I heard a typical bit of Israeli black humor on television. A comedian was recounting a dialogue in the classroom of a religious school where pupils were being taught how to pronounce the word "democracy"—*democratia* in Hebrew.

"Uh . . . democraphia? . . . demografia? . . . democrakia? . . ."

"Sorry, but the origin of the word cannot be traced," the teacher finally announced. "OK, next week we will study the Nine Commandments."

I could not help laughing. Recognizing the absurdity of life is also a way of surviving.

V

Strong Enough for Peace

SEPTEMBER 13, 1993, will always be remembered as the day that Saba and Yasir Arafat shook hands before the world. But the ceremony at the White House in Washington almost did not take place.

Only four days before the signing of the Declaration of Principles that set the stage for Palestinian autonomy, Grandpa was in Jerusalem and Arafat was at the PLO headquarters in Tunisia. And only then, at the last minute, did Arafat send Grandpa the PLO's letter renouncing terrorism and recognizing Israel's right to exist. When he read it, Saba could not resist reacting with irony.

"Now Arafat has the same problem as I have," he said.

And it was true. For some Palestinians, Arafat had capitulated; and for some Israelis, Rabin had capitulated. Naturally I did not agree. Saba had always taught me that you must be strong enough to wage war in order to make peace.

But still it was not easy for him. He had always distrusted Arafat. He probably continued to do so. How can a former soldier trust a former terrorist? They had even fought each other, Saba leading a regular army, Arafat organizing ambushes from clandestine hideouts. Unsurprisingly, Israelis, who had always known Arafat as a terrorist, also had trouble seeing him differently.

But Saba had yet another saying, which was to prove most useful to him:

"You negotiate peace with your enemies, not with your friends."

At times, I think, he needed to convince himself.

"This man is not my friend," he would say. "Arafat is my enemy, with whom I must make peace for the sake of Israel."

But even if peace was possible, could Grandpa ever agree to shake a hand stained with the blood of Jews?

On the day of the signing in Washington, I was at home with a friend of Mom's and a girlfriend, while Jonathan was in the army. It was a hot morning in Washington and it was a hot afternoon in Tel Aviv. The streets were deserted. Like most Israelis, we were watching the ceremony on television. We were of course more nervous than most. We watched Grandpa and Arafat come out of the White House with President Clinton. Grandpa had a half-smile playing on his lips. I caught a glimpse of Grandma on the screen, and she looked resplendent.

There were speeches. Then Grandpa spoke, movingly, eloquently. I will always remember his words:

"We who have fought against you, the Palestinians, we say to you today in a loud and clear voice: Enough of blood and tears. Enough. We harbor no hatred towards you. We have no desire for revenge. We, like you, are people who want to build a home, plant a tree, love, live side by side with you—in dignity, in empathy, as human beings, as free men. We are today giving peace a chance and saying to you: Enough."

He then quoted a verse from Ecclesiastes:

" 'To every thing there is a season, and a time to every purpose under the heaven:

" 'A time to be born, and a time to die . . . A time to kill, and a time to heal . . . A time to weep, and a time to laugh . . . A time to love, and a time to hate; a time of war, and a time of peace.'

"Ladies and gentlemen, the time for peace has come."

Even now when the speech is rebroadcast on television, I repeat the words with him, my voice mixing with his: "Enough of blood and tears."

On that day, though, after the documents were signed, the question on everyone's mind was: Will Rabin shake Arafat's hand?

Of course, he had to. It was more than a matter of protocol. It was the symbolic gesture that the entire world was waiting for. We all knew about his inner ambivalences, and we urged him on. When he seemed to hesitate, in my mind I pleaded with him: Please, Saba, please.

For a few seconds, the world stood still. Clinton seemed to encourage Grandpa with a movement of his body; Arafat was waiting, aware that with one handshake he would go from terrorist to peacemaker in the eyes of much of the world. But all the weight of Israel's tortured history suddenly seemed to hang on Grandpa's shoulders. I could see it in his eyes. It took a gigantic effort for him to believe that Israel's history could be different.

Finally, Grandpa reached out and took Arafat's hand. I cannot say he "stretched" out, because his arm remained slightly doubled, as if he still could not go all the way. But it was enough. Standing behind Grandpa and Arafat, Clinton raised his arms, beaming like a champion boxer, almost like a proud father. In our home in Herzelia, thousands of miles away, we were overcome with delight and relief. Even those who opposed the agreement knew that peace now had a chance.

I HAD a silly thought. Though I inherited my hands from Grandpa, I do not like them. They are small, with stubby fingers and a generous sprinkling of freckles. I often hide them, all the more so because I bite my fingernails when I am nervous. But now his hands, or at least his right hand, had become part of history. And I felt I owed him an apology.

*My grandfather Yitzhak Rabin, at the age of five, with his
Russian-born mother, Rosa, and his younger sister, Rachel, in
1927 (above), and during his service in the Palmach, the secret
Zionist fighting force, before Israel's independence.*

*My grandmother, the former Leah Schlossberg, and her husband,
Yitzhak, not long after their marriage in August 1948.*

My grandfather with my mother, Dalia, in 1953.

Former Prime Minister David Ben-Gurion admired my grandfather and promised that he would become chief of staff. That came to pass in 1964.

My grandfather accepted an honorary degree at Hebrew University for his role in the Israeli victory in the Six-Day War in 1967. Whenever he talked to me about the war, he tended to concentrate on the tank formations rather than on his specific role.

My grandfather playing his beloved game.

*The proud grandfather.
I was two months old when
this photograph was taken in
May 1977.*

*With my brother, Jonathan,
age five (I was three).*

Avi Pelossof, my stepfather, and my mother in 1985, three years after they met. They were married in 1987.

One of the few recent photographs of us together, at a fashion show in Caesarea in 1995.

I entered the army in 1995, for two years of military service.

© Angeli Agency

The funeral. From left: Uncle Yuval, Grandma, me, my mother and Jonathan.

King Hussein of Jordan and my grandmother in December 1995 at a ceremony in Tel Aviv renaming the hospital where my grandfather died. It is now called the Yitzhak Rabin Trauma Center.

At a Jerusalem event marking the end of the thirty-day mourning period.

That night, I spoke to Mom and Grandma on the telephone. They talked effusively about the speech, about the ceremony, about the reactions of all the people who were there, about how Grandpa was feeling, about the tie he was wearing, and about all the things, big and small, that families talk about when they are on opposite sides of the globe.

When Grandpa returned, his reaction was characteristically undramatic; there was a shyness about him even in moments of glory:

"I have received so many honors in my life, I have lived so many extraordinary situations, that I thought it impossible to go any further . . . and yet . . ."

The road to the White House lawn had indeed been long. He had climbed from freedom fighter in the Palmach, to general, to army chief of staff, to ambassador to the United States, to Prime Minister. Then he had fallen and had had to start again. But he never gave up, even in the face of setbacks. And that was one of the lessons he passed on to me. If I was disappointed because something had not worked out the way I had hoped, he would say:

"It's not serious, Noale. Things always turn out for the best. You'll do better next time."

He always managed to believe there would be a "next time."

In 1990, he decided to challenge Shimon Peres for the leadership of the Labor Party. With polls showing that he was popular and Peres was in trouble, Grandpa thought that, as Labor leader, he could reorganize the party and perhaps even force early elections. He therefore proposed a new vote for the leadership.

But it was not enough just to propose a new vote. The party first had to vote to decide whether to advance the party primary or to hold it, as scheduled, a year or so later. And Peres opposed an early primary because he understood his position to be vulnerable. It was a hard-fought battle, and Peres won. Grandpa returned home with a handful of close allies, looking defeated. We ordered pizzas, but they tasted bitter mixed with our tears. To this day, my family refers to the occasion as the Pizza Evening.

For a second time in thirteen years, many Israelis thought Saba's career as a public figure was over.

ONE DAY Avi announced at breakfast:

"I dreamed last night that Saba had become Prime Minister."

We looked at him as if he had gone crazy, but soon thereafter, in February 1992, Saba surprised us again, this time by winning the Labor leadership when the party primary was finally held. Apart from Saba and Peres, there were two other candidates who were not expected to win, but either of them could nonetheless have prevented one or the other of the frontrunners from winning the required minimum of 40 percent of the vote. I remember the nerve-racking evening we spent while the votes were being counted. Family and close friends had gathered in my grandparents' apartment in Ramat Aviv. The tension was unbearable. The radio was broadcasting the ballot count, and the lead kept swinging back and forth. One minute Saba was ahead, the next minute Peres had a small advantage.

In the early hours of the morning, Saba announced that he was going to rest. Everyone was taken aback that he could think of resting at such a moment. We were on tenterhooks. But, in truth, he did not have a nap. After about ten minutes, I took three glasses of whiskey into his bedroom and I signaled Jonathan to follow me. With Saba stretched out on his bed and my brother and me sitting beside him, we drank and chatted about everyday things. He was so calm that later we decided he had been confident of victory all along. But in fact he won by a cat's whisker, with just 40.5 percent of the vote (Peres registered 35 percent). When the final results came through, at about two-thirty a.m., we all headed over to Labor Party headquarters. What a celebration we had that night!

It was a year of many celebrations. On March 1, my parents threw a party at our house in Herzelia to celebrate Grandpa's seventieth birthday. We decorated the house with photographs of him at all stages of his life, and dozens of his friends joined the family for the occasion. Then there was election night, in June. This time family and friends gathered around Grandpa at his apartment to watch the results coming in on television. It too was a tight race. I remember the sound of cheers echoing across the neighborhood when it was finally announced that the Labor Party had come out on top. We all went to the Dan Hotel in Tel Aviv, where we savored the sweet taste of victory with friends and supporters into the early hours of the morning.

So Avi's dream had come true.

AFTER that, as they say, the rest was history. Grandpa had the slimmest of majorities in the Knesset, but he nonetheless initiated the reversal of the settlements policy with the full backing of the Labor Party. Crucially, Grandpa and Peres went from being competitors to being friends and allies. Grandpa authorized the opening of secret negotiations with the PLO, but it was Peres, as the new foreign minister, who frequently led the Israeli delegation to the talks being held under Norwegian auspices in various locations near Oslo.

When the 1994 Nobel Peace Prize was awarded, no one questioned that Peres should be honored along with Saba and Arafat. Together, all three had fought for peace. And on December 10, 1994, they stood together in Oslo to receive their medals and certificates from the King of Norway: Saba and Peres, formerly political arch-rivals, and Arafat, who barely two years earlier had still been considered a terrorist.

I watched the ceremony on television at home. Grandma, Mom, Avi, Uncle Yuval and his wife had all traveled to Oslo for the occasion. I remember that when Saba had finished his acceptance speech, he turned to the one person whose approval he coveted, and Savta nodded in reply. When the two of them returned to Israel, I had the impression that Savta was prouder of the prize than Saba was. He was pleased that his past efforts had been recognized, but he was aware that much still remained to be done.

WHENEVER Grandpa appeared in public with Arafat, he made a point of looking solemn. He had not forgotten the hundreds of Israelis killed by PLO terrorists. He was uncomfortable about these public appearances together, even if they did make good photo opportunities. He certainly knew that many Israelis would never forgive him if he seemed to befriend Arafat. And he always stressed that the negotiations were between the representatives of two states and not between friends or brothers. If Arafat is sitting across the negotiating table, he would say, it is precisely because he is the enemy.

Yet gradually, confidence began to build between the two men. Grandpa recognized that Arafat was a serious negotiating partner, that his word carried weight. In time, Grandpa went even further, concluding that Arafat was a man of integrity. And for all the stops and starts of the negotiations that followed the White House signing, Grandpa's respect for Arafat continued to grow.

The only time I met the PLO leader was after Saba's death, when he came to my grandparents' apartment to express his condolences to Grandma and the rest of the family. I was eager to meet him. Until then, I had only seen him on television, wearing a military uniform and a kaffiyeh covering his head. Suddenly I saw a man arrive wearing dark glasses, a long woolen overcoat, a hat and a large dark scarf. He was unrecognizable. He looked like a private detective or, at best, like a distant relative who turns up unannounced for a visit.

For security reasons, Arafat had not attended Saba's funeral. His visit to Grandma was also carried out with the utmost secrecy and was announced to the press only after he had left Tel Aviv. Avi was involved in the planning, and he picked up Arafat in a car from the local airport in Tel Aviv.

When he entered the apartment, Arafat kissed everyone—Grandma and Mom were kissed three times on the head, Uncle Yuval was kissed three times on the head and twice on the cheeks, and Jonathan and I too were kissed three times on the head.

"*Shalom,*" I said.

We all sat down, and I studied him carefully to make sure he did not have three eyes, four ears, and little antennas coming out of his head. We had Arafat, "the enemy," in our home. But the man in front of me was courteous, friendly, chatting with ease, even smiling. His voice was calm and gentle. I remembered Grandpa telling us:

"He's really quite nice. . . ."

Mesmerized, I did not say a word throughout the visit except hello—*Shalom*—and goodbye. I was a fascinated witness to a footnote to the history of Israel. There, in Grandpa's own sitting room, surrounded by photographs of him in uniform, by a bust of him, by a certificate of the Nobel Peace Prize, was the PLO leader, who had come to pay homage to his fallen peace partner, to pledge to complete the work they had begun together. I could no longer think of Arafat as a monster. He kept calling Grandma "my sister." That made him my great-uncle.

It was also then that I fully appreciated what Saba had done. He had understood that it was possible to make peace with this man. He had taken the risk, and it had paid off.

WHAT will I inherit from him? I wonder. He had a way with words that did not please everyone. He once gave one of Peres's advisers the nickname "Peres's poodle," and it stuck with the poor man. And he used to liken the settlers who opposed the peace process to "the wings of a propeller, going round and round." Despite the wind they created, he still pressed on with the process.

I think that most of all I would like to have some of Saba's strength—his strength to deal with defeats with courage, his strength to make possible what others can barely imagine. When he was alive, he pointed the way for me. Now that he is gone, I hope his memory will guide me.

VI

There Are No Birds in Auschwitz

THROUGHOUT my schooling, the history of the Jews was presented as an endless litany of suffering and persecution, which climaxed with the Holocaust and Hitler's attempt to exterminate all Jews. It was not easy for a child to understand what a people, my people, could have done to deserve such punishment.

I think I was about five years old when I first saw images of the Holocaust, of the deportation trains, of the emaciated figures found in concentration camps at the end of the war. All the images returned to me in nightmares. They were mostly black-and-white dreams, like the photographs and films I had seen. I was on a train, there was no light, bodies crowded around me, I could not breathe. Everyone else was starving, their bodies naked, their heads shaven, but I was dressed normally. I saw myself in color.

Mom said I kept asking:

"But where was God? Why didn't He do something?"

Children ask impossible questions. I cannot remember what my mother said. I certainly do not know how I would answer those questions today. But somehow, as children, we came to understand that the diaspora, even the Holocaust, was God's way of testing the Jews. If we allowed ourselves to be destroyed, we did not deserve a place on earth. But since we survived against all odds, we had a land, our own land, the state of Israel.

In August 1945, when Israel existed only as a dream, the World Zionist Congress declared:

"What happened to our people in Europe did not happen and could not have happened to any people that had its own country and its own state."

The notion of the survival of the Jews, then, was always central to the very idea of Israel. The Holocaust became a pillar of our national identity. Millions of Jews were exterminated because they had no home of their own. Israel existed to insure that this could never happen again.

April 19, 1993, was the fiftieth anniversary of the uprising of the Jews trapped in the Warsaw ghetto. Grandpa was invited to Poland to attend events marking the milestone. It would be his first visit to Poland, and the first visit there by an Israeli Prime Minister.

Poland has always been a deep wound in the Jewish memory. During World War II, three million Jews, many deported from other parts of Europe, died in Poland's death camps. At the time of the German invasion of Poland in September 1939, more than 400,000 Jews lived in Warsaw alone. And within a year, they were driven into a ghetto that was sealed with a ten-foot-high wall. By the end of 1941, at least 50,000 Jews had died of hunger and disease inside the ghetto. Then, in June 1942, mass deportations began, and within six months, some 300,000 of Warsaw's Jews had been put to death in Treblinka. Early in 1943, the Nazis announced plans to destroy the ghetto.

On April 19, 1943, the day before Hitler's birthday, a few hundred men, most of them young, staged an uprising, using weapons smuggled in by the Polish Resistance. There were still around 60,000 Jews inside the ghetto, and many fought bravely, even with their bare hands, but they stood no chance against Nazi power. Over a period of three weeks, the Nazis advanced, burning house by house, until most of the leaders of the rebellion were cornered and chose suicide over capture. Then, for good measure, the Nazi commander ordered the destruction of the Tlomackie Synagogue. Of the handful of brave Jewish fighters who survived, a half-dozen are still alive today.

So it was both courage and brutality that would be remembered on the fiftieth anniversary of the uprising.

Grandpa was to be accompanied by an official delegation, and when the education minister announced that she would be taking her granddaughter, Saba replied:

"I'll take mine along too."

Except for Grandma and Mom, he rarely invited family members to join him on official trips, but this was a special occasion. At the age of sixteen, I was old enough to understand the significance of the trip, both as the anniversary of the uprising and as the first visit to Poland by an Israeli Prime Minister. Grandma was of course also part of the delegation.

Strangely, until then, Saba and I had never discussed the Holocaust. Since both his and Grandma's parents had come to Palestine in the 1920s, we had no close relatives who had died at the hands of the Nazis. In my house there was no display of prewar photographs of lost great-aunts or -uncles who died in the Holocaust. My knowledge of the Shoa came from school and documentaries, but not from the direct testimonies of survivors.

Those who did survive and reached Israel after the war often had difficulty talking about what had happened. Even as they tried to build a new life, many experienced guilt for having survived when the rest of their families were wiped out, asking themselves, "Why me? Why not them?"

For my generation, though, the Holocaust was less real. I even thought of my trip to Poland as a sort of school project. I would take photographs, perhaps take notes. I would finally put in context the dreadful images that haunted my childhood dreams. And we would

show the Poles that we Jews were different today. I
imagined myself telling them:

"Look at us. We're not the defenseless little Jews that
you allowed to be massacred. We are Israelis. We're not
dead. We're alive, strong and proud."

And in the end, that is what I felt.

But the trip also made the Holocaust seem more real
to me than ever before.

The first day in Warsaw was oddly unmoving. With
crowds of journalists and television crews trailing
Grandpa and Grandma, we visited Poland's Tomb of
the Unknown Soldier, a huge mausoleum that was a
typical example of how totalitarian regimes invest in
symbols and not people. At the tomb, there was a
military guard of honor made up of young Polish soldiers with sharp Aryan features and blond hair. They
wore pressed uniforms and long boots, and their guns
with fixed bayonets were drawn in salute. It was quite
impressive.

Yet I felt slightly uneasy. True, they were only "toy
soldiers" used for parades, but in my eyes they represented an Aryan fighting force that could suddenly turn
its swords on the Jews. Why should I feel threatened?
Two generations had passed since the Holocaust. I was
raised in an independent Israel. These soldiers were
there to honor us, but instead they disturbed me. Perhaps it was the harshness of the place: a grim monument
in grim weather.

Next we visited various sites linked to the Jews of Warsaw, including Umschlagplatz, where Jews were loaded onto trains on their way to Treblinka, and the home of Mordechai Anielewicz, head of the Eyal, the Jewish acronym for the combat force that led the ghetto uprising. But all we saw were buildings put up after the war to replace those destroyed by the Nazis. It seemed to me to be no more emotional than the annual Holocaust Day ceremonies at school. I thought to myself, Why did I have to come all the way here in order to feel nothing? Grandpa and Grandma promised me the next day would be different.

That evening, we attended the main ceremony marking the Warsaw uprising. The Polish President, Lech Walesa, was there, along with dignitaries from around the world, including the American Vice-President, Al Gore. Grandpa was, of course, a guest of honor. There were speeches, as well as an audiovisual show that was meant to illustrate the uprising for us. Again, I was not impressed. Nothing could persuade me that it represented something that had really happened there. It was just another ceremony to remember the Holocaust, no more.

But the next day *was* different.

It began with a tour of the Jewish cemetery in Warsaw. Many old and impressive graves, which carry quotations from poets and philosophers, testify to the education and sophistication of Warsaw's Jews before the war. Time has not erased their beauty. Then there is a mass grave in which uncounted numbers of Jewish victims of murder, starvation and illness are buried together. These were people who died even before being sent to a death camp. And they are remembered in a statue that shows Janus Korchak and children from his orphanage who were killed by the Nazis. All this began to make clear to me how the Jewish community in Poland had been decimated.

Then we went to Auschwitz.

From my childhood, the very word "Auschwitz" had come to symbolize one of the blackest moments in Jewish history. At school, we had learned how it operated. It was built on Himmler's order of April 27, 1940, as a KZ, a concentration camp. Later, another camp, Birkenau, was built nearby, supposedly as an industrial installation to make synthetic rubber. But the only thing that was truly industrialized was death. There were five gas chambers in all at the Auschwitz complex—"shower rooms," they called them—and five crematoriums. There was a lake where the victims' ashes were thrown and a warehouse where their clothes were stored.

In true Nazi fashion, everything was worked out in coldly efficient detail. Those who could not work were sent straight to the gas chambers and then cremated in the ovens; the rest worked until they dropped and then either died of exhaustion or were killed. In the hospital, Joseph Mengele, the "angel of death," carried out medical experiments on children, usually twins. But the Nazis were also romantics, we were taught. Sometimes they picked their victims to the sound of arias from *Tosca*.

All this I knew. Now I would see and feel it for myself.

It was a cold, misty day. We flew to Krakow and were then driven in a convoy of buses to Auschwitz. On the way, we passed through villages where peasants recognized our Israeli flags and waved cheerfully, as if we were in a circus parade rather than on a pilgrimage to a place of death. Samuel Gogol, an Auschwitz survivor, watched them through the window.

"To hell with them," he said with disgust. "When the deportation trains came through here, no one waved. No one said a word."

The road passed through beautiful countryside, and I kept thinking, How could the most disgusting events in the history of mankind take place in such pastoral surroundings?

Grandpa had invited a number of other survivors of the Polish horror to accompany us. They were submerged in dark memories. During the bus ride, I sat beside Shevach Weiss, a Holocaust survivor who is the Speaker of the Knesset. Also on board was Menachem Stern, a doctor and an officer in the Israeli army. During the war, he was luckier than most. His family was hidden by a Polish family and escaped being rounded up. But he still remembers Poland with bitterness.

After the war, he and his family were leaving Poland by train. When they reached the frontier, Polish soldiers forced them to strip to be searched for "stolen" objects. And to this day, he can remember the soldiers kicking and stamping on his family with hate in their eyes. But now the terrified little Jewish boy had returned to Poland in the uniform of an Israeli army officer. And he fulfilled his dream of being saluted by a Polish officer. It was a victory for him, but also for all Jews who had known similar humiliation.

When we reached the camp, I noticed that the village of Auschwitz is nearby. What could the villagers have thought when they saw the trains arriving, crowded with desperate people? This area is also very green, with woods near the camp. But I was struck by the silence. Fifty years later, birds still do not sing in Auschwitz. Was it just my impression? No, other people noticed the same thing: there are no birds in Auschwitz.

We entered through an iron gate under a Nazi sign that reads *Arbeit Macht Frei* (Work Will Make You Free). It was of course a lie to deceive the deportees into thinking they were arriving at a labor camp. Many probably never saw the sign in the dark. And if they did see it, they most likely did not notice that the *b* in *Arbeit* had been written upside down. The prisoners who had been forced to make the sign had inverted the letter on purpose to warn newcomers that something was wrong. Yet, even if the new arrivals had spotted this mistake and understood its hidden message, they had no choice but to go through the gates.

I thought of the Jews arriving here, hungry and ill from the journey, with barely a stitch of clothes to keep them warm. I was wearing three layers of clothing against the wintery cold, and I still felt the chill.

The tour began in a room full of documents and photographs recording the horror. One photograph showed a young woman surrounded by laughing Nazi soldiers. She held a sign in her hand, which read: "I am a pig Jewish whore." Another photograph showed an elderly rabbi having his beard shaved off by other soldiers.

Next we saw a "model room," with an iron bed, pajamas, a rusty iron bedpan, an old wooden desk, and a chair. My imagination was working overtime. Everything was becoming too real. I almost choked with emotion.

We then stood beside a red brick wall, the "death wall" where hundreds of people were brought daily and executed without reason. We said Kaddish, the prayer for the dead. It was a very sad moment. Everyone was upset, including my grandparents. I had a knot in my stomach. Many survivors were weeping.

We moved to another section, where there was a succession of macabre window displays. Behind the first glass window we saw thousands of toothbrushes, shoe brushes, shaving brushes, hairbrushes and cleaning brushes. All brushes, yet each of them different. Just like the prisoners: all Jews, yet every one an individual, with a separate life.

Another window was filled with thousands upon thousands of eyeglass frames. I could see the eyes behind each pair of glasses, dried-out eyes with their pupils torn from them. Just thinking of those eyes made me feel ill. I looked over at Grandpa. He was concentrating, asking questions. He wanted to know every detail. When were the glasses collected? Were they taken from victims before or after their death? It was Saba's own way of dealing with it all. He needed to know everything.

We walked past still more windows filled with hellish mementos: broken dolls, a bloodstained pacifier, suitcases with names, a pot filled with human ashes. Human beings are very small, but their lives are very big. When we passed a window full of shoes, everything came into horrible focus for me. For each pair of shoes, there was a pair of feet; each pair of feet had a body, and each body had a soul. It was then that I understood that the Holocaust was not just about death; it was about six million lives. Tears filled my eyes, but I could not cry. I was in shock.

From there we went to Birkenau, the Auschwitz annex.

The railroad tracks end at this camp, as if one needed reminding that this was indeed the end for people arriving here. To one side there were low huts made of stone;

on the other side, they were made of wood. Most of the wooden huts had been burned at the end of the war; where they were destroyed, all that remained standing were two naked stone chimneys. Many of the huts had housed women. You cannot say women "lived" here, because scores were crowded into each tiny hut and were forced to sleep in narrow bunk beds hardly bigger than a drawer. Beyond these buildings stood the remains of one crematorium. It was bombed from the air by the Allies, and it was not rebuilt. It was there that we held a brief religious service.

Samuel Gogol had promised to play the harmonica at the ceremony, because it was a harmonica that saved his life in Auschwitz. His parents died in a car accident when he was young, and he was left at Janus Korchak's orphanage because his grandmother could not take care of him. But one night before the orphanage was wiped out by the Nazis, Korchak insisted that Gogol's grandmother take him and that they go into hiding. However, Korchak's plan came too late: they were denounced to the Nazis by Polish "friends" and were sent to Auschwitz.

"When we got there, we were separated," Gogol recounted to me during our trip, "old women and children to one side, people who could work to the other side. My grandmother was condemned to death. But I stood on my toes to make myself seem taller and was chosen for work. Otherwise they'd have killed me along with the other children.

"I was able to keep my harmonica, and I would play it softly at night," he went on. "It was the only thing that stopped me from going mad. Then, one night, I could not find it. Could it have been stolen? A few days later, I saw it in the hands of another prisoner, an old man who was asleep. I woke him and offered him one week of my food rations if he would return it to me. That's how I got it back."

Some time later, a Nazi officer who was impressed by Gogol's musical skills recruited him as a new member of the "orchestra of death." This was another invention of those "romantic" Nazis—an orchestra of Jews who would play while other Jews were led to their deaths.

"I saw others pass, knowing they were going to die, but I could say nothing," he remembered. "I had to play or else I would be sent to join them, but I could not look them in the eyes. So I played with my eyes closed. And since then I have always played my harmonica with my eyes closed."

He told his story quickly, as if he did not want to impose the full weight of his pain. He did not talk about the liberation of the camp, of his later life. His memories were all enclosed in his harmonica. And when he played it, they came rushing back.

This time he had promised to play with his eyes open. His touching, melancholic music made many of us cry. Even Grandpa seemed close to weeping. However, fifty years on, among friends, Gogol still could not open his eyes.

On the flight home, many of the survivors thanked Grandpa for restoring Jewish honor. When it was Gogol's turn, he said:

"Thank you for enabling me to return to hell as a proud Jew, as a citizen of a free nation, of a nation with a great leader."

Grandpa smiled and blushed a little.

Gogol said he could now die in peace. He had closed the circle of his life. And just one month later, he passed away. For another man in the delegation, Simcha Holtzberg, who lost his entire family in the Holocaust, the visit was also to be the culmination of his life. Soon after returning to Israel, he too died.

I also thanked Saba. The trip had made me see, hear and feel things that had never before been clear to me. Only after Auschwitz did I understand the power of silent memories. Only as I struggle to describe my reactions do I understand that some events are, literally, beyond words. I only hope that my friends, that other young Israelis, can also travel to Auschwitz to hear the silence. In this way, we will never forget what the survivors can never forget.

I think that for a long time survivors remained silent, prisoners of their suffering, because they felt no one wanted to hear their stories. A telephone hot line, run by an organization called Amcha, now exists to listen to them. If survivors cannot sleep, if they are awakened by nightmares, they can call the special number. They can talk about the family members they lost, they can wonder aloud if they could have done anything to save them, they can ask why they are still alive. And many do.

I can understand that many survivors feel lonely. My generation of Israeli-born Sabras, for whom Arabs were the enemy, not Germans, has little time for the Holocaust. We rarely talk about it among ourselves. For example, we know that in the 1960s Adolf Eichmann was kidnapped in Argentina, brought back to Israel for trial, and executed for crimes against humanity. But that was long before we were born.

Occasionally, that past returns to the headlines. In the 1980s, John Demjanjuk, the man thought to be the butcher of Treblinka, was extradited from the United States to face trial here. The trial in Jerusalem lasted seven years, and to everyone's astonishment, he was eventually acquitted. Many witnesses recognized him, but doubts about his identity remained, and that was enough. For the Israel of today, respect for democracy and justice is more important than any exercise in revenge.

The Holocaust may belong to history, but it was the price we paid to become a nation. Auschwitz was like a cradle of death that enabled future generations of Israelis to live. And if those who went through that hell on earth cannot speak, we must learn to listen to their silence. They have a right to be heard. They are telling us that this must never happen again, that Jews should never again lower their heads and be led to the slaughter. They are telling us we must never forget.

VII

Grandpa's Ambassador

FOR THE past twenty years, groups of young Israelis have been traveling abroad to learn about other countries and, perhaps more important, to inform young people in other lands about Israel. These delegations are organized jointly by the ministry of education and the foreign ministry. In February 1994, I qualified through oral and written examinations as one of sixty-four teenagers to be dispatched around the world. My group, three boys and three girls, was earmarked for Britain. I was going as Noa, an Israeli teenager, and not as Prime Minister Rabin's granddaughter.

Before we left, we attended two week-long seminars in Jerusalem, where we were briefed on the country we would be visiting and on the kind of questions we might be asked, and we were given basic information about Israel that might be useful. Fortunately, we were not expected to be polished diplomats. The idea was for us to

visit schools and talk to groups of students about our country in a language they could relate to.

We traveled in pairs. My partner was Dan Arad, and luckily we got on very well. At first, I found it quite intimidating to address a crowd of as many as one hundred twenty students. But since we had been well prepared during the seminars and my adrenaline was pumping, I managed to hold my own.

Dan and I tried to make our prepared remarks about our country and our way of life sound more like a conversation than a lecture. We were not there to preach. This approach seemed to suit most audiences. The students asked few questions about politics and were more interested in discovering how different we were from them.

"What music do you like? What are your teachers like at school? At what age can you drive? At what age can you drink beer? Do you have McDonald's and Coca-Cola in Israel? What do you do on weekends? Do you go to church?"

It gradually dawned on us that English teenagers knew very little about Israel. Or, rather, that what they knew was wrong. Many seemed to imagine that Israel was the size of Africa, that we traveled on camels, that we all carried guns, that we were all very religious. I found this caricature amusing. It was as if we were living in the Middle Ages.

Dan and I quickly realized that we had to start from the beginning or else our audience would not have a proper understanding of our country. It was quite a test for us to put everything into context—and not to forget any important aspects of our culture.

We began by explaining that Israel was the land of the Jews, but that these Jews had come from many countries and had brought with them different languages and cultures. So we had needed a national language and had chosen Hebrew. It was the ancient language of the Jews, we said, but it had almost disappeared. It was hardly being spoken anywhere fifty years ago. Now every Israeli speaks it. Of course, we have had to assimilate many modern technical and scientific terms. But we even have our own slang now.

We found it more difficult to explain that Israel is in a way divided into two societies, religious and secular, old and new, traditional and fashionable. It was hard to get this across because Western countries are much more homogeneous. Teenagers in these countries tend to dress the same, eat the same food, listen to the same music, have a similar education. In Israel, two worlds live side by side.

I think a lot of young people in the West must have trouble understanding how Israel can be a modern democracy and a religious state at the same time. We have very religious people whose entire lives are ruled by the Torah, a sacred scripture. We respect the Sabbath every Saturday more than people in the West seem to respect their Sabbath on Sunday. During Yom Kippur, our Day of Atonement, everything stops, including traffic and radio and television broadcasts. It is a day of penitence and fasting.

We would also explain that for us the Bible is not just a religious text; it also records the history of the Jewish people, is a work of great literature, and contains a mine of information about a whole range of subjects.

Then, before the young audiences could become bored, we would remind them of the other side of Israel, the modern Western side, to which we belonged. Yes, we go to cinemas, theaters, good restaurants; yes, we hang out in lively cafés where we drink Coke, have snacks and gossip. We like dancing to the latest sounds, we watch MTV, we wear the current fashions and we stay out late.

"Just like you," we would say.

Still, the preparation we underwent before talking in public about Israel made me realize as never before that I live in a land full of contradictions. Thanks to our excellent telecommunications, the telephone company has installed a fax near the Wailing Wall. Instead of coming in person, as thousands of people do every year, to place a written prayer or wish to God in a crevice in this sacred wall, today you can send your message by fax from wherever you are in the world. A company employee is then charged with placing your message in a crevice, on your behalf. Likewise, we have the glass-fronted modern buildings of Tel Aviv and, not many miles away, we have the ancient stone city of Jerusalem. Hebrew is our official language, but one is as likely to hear Russian, English, Spanish, Greek and of course Arabic on our streets.

"Why do you do military service?" we were often asked.

This was the major difference between us and English teenagers. Mandatory military service was abolished in Britain in the 1950s, so the students found it odd that, while they might take a year off between school and college to wander the world, we all joined the army.

"Boys now do thirty-two months of military service and girls do seventeen months," I said. "You'd be surprised, but we don't mind joining up because it is a quick way of growing up and it gives us time to think about what we want to do in life."

We explained that we could often choose what we did in the army. In my case, I was hoping to work in some area of communications, as I was already taking courses in this field in school.

"And, no, we're not bloodthirsty soldiers who sleep with guns by our side," I would say, invariably provoking laughter. "We do learn about using a rifle, but we're also taught some first aid, general information and, most of all, discipline."

We would also stress that the army is a way of bringing us together as a country.

"We're such a melting pot of people with different origins that the army is a bit like a mold that gives us a common identity."

"What's the exact difference between a Jew and an Israeli?"

"There are Jews all over the world, like there are Christians and Muslims everywhere, but the Israelis live in Israel," I replied. "But even in Israel there are Jewish Israelis, Muslim Israelis, Christian Israelis and even Israelis with no religion at all."

It was strange. I felt I knew a lot about young English people's lives and they knew nothing about us. We had been prepared in advance that that would be the case. But I realized now how much patience was required to be an ambassador.

Dan and I thought it was particularly important to make clear to our audiences just how small Israel is. Only in this way could they appreciate Israel's geographical vulnerability. And it would help them to understand why Israel had so often found itself at war with its neighbors.

Our preferred technique was simple. When we could, we would hold up a map of Israel and the Middle East and point to Israel.

"Israel is as big as Wales," I would say, "but it has only half the population of London. So imagine half the Londoners spread across Wales and there you have Israel. We have mountains and beaches. In winter, we can ski in the morning, and six hours away by car, we can sunbathe in the afternoon.

"Now if you look at a map of the world, you'll see that all the Arab countries together cover an area the size of the United States. Then take Wales and compare. So it's as if the United States was surrounding and threatening Wales. That's why we feel so small and exposed and have to be ready to defend ourselves."

WHEN we had left Israel, we had been promised a quiet trip. It was not to be. The morning after we landed in London, devastating news reached us from home. And it filled the headlines of all English newspapers.

On February 25, 1994, Baruch Goldstein, a member of the extreme right-wing militant group Kach, entered the Tomb of the Patriarchs in Hebron and opened fire on Muslim worshippers celebrating Ramadan. More than forty people were killed and scores more were wounded.

Hebron, on the West Bank, is one of the oldest towns on earth. And on its hillside stands the Tomb of the Patriarchs, which is holy to Jew and Muslim alike. At the tomb, a mosque was built on top of an ancient synagogue, and since the Six-Day War of 1967, both religions have had access to the shrine. But instead of being a place that united Jews and Muslims, the shrine was a source of tension between extremists on both sides. Israeli soldiers have patrolled the Hebron area since it was retaken in 1967, and after the Intifada, it became impossible for cars with Israeli license plates to pass through there without being stoned. Hebron became an arena for repeated confrontations between Jews and Muslims, between Israeli soldiers and Arab youths.

But what had happened now was unthinkable. This was not a question of Arabs or Jews. It was a massacre of the innocents.

Rioting had immediately erupted in Hebron, Arafat had called an urgent meeting of the United Nations Security Council, and the peace talks were thrown into jeopardy.

Grandpa was devastated. He said the killings had made him ashamed to be an Israeli.

But what was I going to do? How was I going to explain to young English men and women why an Israeli madman had opened fire on a group of Arabs in the middle of their Friday prayers? I knew exactly how Grandpa felt, but I could not use the same language. I was now a diplomat. I could not just say, I am ashamed to be an Israeli. I had to try to explain.

"There are maniacs on both sides who will do any-thing to stop the peace process," I would say. "The Pales-tinian extremists want to create a Muslim, Jewish-free state in Palestine, while Israeli extremists feel they have a Biblical right to the very land on which the Palestinians lay their claim. Both factions fight to destroy a peace process which is all about recognizing the respective states and the rights of their citizens. The price of peace is reconciliation and compromise. If we believe in it, we cannot allow the extremists to succeed."

I realized then that I would not make a good politician. My explanation made me feel too uncomfortable. I wanted Israel to look good in the eyes of the world, but I also had to be honest. I must admit that I found it difficult to discuss politics with the English we met.

"What is a democratic country doing occupying another country anyway?" we were once asked.

"The idea of the war in 1967 was not to occupy lands," Dan said. "We had to defend ourselves and the occupation was the consequence of this."

"But we have already withdrawn from some land and we're negotiating the return of other occupied areas," I added.

It must have been more difficult for earlier delegations, the members of which could not fall back on the peace process to demonstrate Israel's goodwill. Now, at least, we seemed more sympathetic because we were ready to make concessions. But Dan and I still faced some tricky moments.

I remember visiting one school in London's East End where a young Catholic boy had clearly come prepared to embarrass us. He had a list of questions that he challenged us with:

"Why did you invade Lebanon and kill thousands of people? Why have you closed the university in Gaza at least thirty times?..."

He had done his homework very well. We tried to deal with his questions one by one.

"The war in Lebanon was terrible and it divided many Israelis, but our kibbutzes and villages in the north were being rocketed from Lebanon. We couldn't just stand by and do nothing. We have a right to live and work in peace."

The boy, who was certainly a strong anti-Zionist, became angry, as if he wanted to turn the debate into a personal quarrel. He did not seem to care about our answers.

"What right have you to seize these lands?" he insisted. "I won't say 'Biblical' lands because you are not even religious."

I admit that at that point I was relieved that the person escorting us from the Israeli embassy in London leaned across and whispered:

"Tell him to study his own history. If he looks under B, for Balfour, he will read the Balfour Declaration of November 2, 1917, and he will find his reply."

It was in this document that the British government promised the Jewish people a "national home" in Palestine.

I hope I did not make enemies in England. I certainly made many friends. When I returned home, Grandpa asked me for my reactions. But instead of giving a serious ambassador's answer to his Prime Minister, I dwelled on the fun we had had and not on the political debates.

"Have you tried eating some of their food? Thank goodness there were plenty of McDonald's around," I told him.

He laughed heartily at his little ambassador.

WHILE I was away, a huge peace rally in Tel Aviv brought together more than fifty thousand young Israelis and Arabs. It was very important because it helped to breathe life back into the peace talks after the Hebron massacre. The situation in Hebron, though, was still difficult. The Israeli army had been authorized to fire on armed Jewish settlers, foreign observers had been sent to Hebron to monitor the situation, and Hamas terrorists had killed seven Israelis in Galilee in reprisal. But the peace talks had resumed. Neither Grandpa nor Arafat wanted to break them off.

Saba was incredibly busy those days. We had to watch television just to know where he was: one day in Moscow, the next day on the West Bank, that evening in the Knesset. He never stopped.

I remember a trip he made to Cairo to negotiate with Arafat over the borders of Gaza and Jericho, which would become part of the new Palestinian autonomous state. The two delegations had reached agreement, but Grandpa was still not ready to sign. He studied the maps for one hour with the care of a scientist. How could he not have had mixed feelings? Gaza is just a strip of desert, but it is where Samson died. And Jericho has been part of Jewish history since time immemorial. Finally, he signed. Two months later, the Palestinian flag was flying over Gaza and then, a few days later, over Jericho.

It was a moment of great significance because, for the first time, the Declaration of Principles signed in Washington had changed the situation on the ground. For Palestinians, it was proof that Israel was sincere in its desire for peace. And for Israelis, it was evidence that the peace process was fast becoming irreversible.

WHETHER I liked it or not, I was always "Rabin's granddaughter." I couldn't let down my guard. Friends of mine would sometimes tease me, saying that if they were the Prime Minister's granddaughter, they would use their family ties to win special privileges. But this was not my way of thinking. I tried hard to be simply Noa; although I could not, and did not, want to forget who my grandfather was, I wished that others would.

After the trip to England, I was asked to give an interview to *Yediot Aharonot,* a leading Israeli newspaper, about our delegation's experience. I was not required to do so, but I had felt very involved in the trip and thought it might interest young Israelis. So I did so quite willingly. The article, headlined "I am more to the left than my grandfather," backfired on me. Although I was not criticized directly, some people gave me secondhand reports of what others thought. "She talks of feminism, but how can she consider herself a feminist when her grandmother is not one?" for example.

I was annoyed. I knew that had I not been the "granddaughter of," I would probably not have been asked to give the interview in the first place. And yet by the same token, I had wanted to be listened to as Noa and judged as Noa. I did not want to put my whole family on trial.

When I told Grandpa about this incident, he was, as usual, the voice of reason.

"When will you learn that you cannot please everyone, Noa? You should learn to ignore comments like this. You only encourage people if you show that you're angry."

Teachers often seemed to expect a lot from me—or at least they made it sound as if they did. I remember during classes dealing with current affairs that some teachers made a habit of announcing at the beginning of the lesson, "Although we have the Prime Minister's granddaughter here, you must not feel embarrassed about expressing your opinion." Obviously, this statement had the reverse effect: With a room full of eyes focused on me, I was the one who felt embarrassed. For the first part of the lesson, I would keep quiet, not wanting to draw any more attention upon myself. Then, after a while, I would start to relax, and invariably, I would be unable to resist expressing my opinion. If the government was involved, I would make a point, whenever possible, of referring to the specific minister whose ministry was responsible for the specific area of the debate. I would make reference to the Prime Minister or defense minister only when I had no alternative. But I was never comfortable doing so.

I hate hypocrites. I am always wary of people's motives and of what they might be saying behind my back. Once Saba was Prime Minister, I tried hard to show that I had not become a self-important little snob. But it hurt me when people did not accept me for myself. I had to keep reminding myself of Grandpa's advice:

"Noa, don't worry about what people say about you, particularly if they don't know you."

He had learned long ago that you cannot please everyone, above all if you are a politician. When he was attacked in the press and in the Knesset, he would wave his hand in a familiar sign of indifference, as if to say:

"It doesn't matter so long as I know what I am doing."

And he always did. He was not a politician who was eager for praise and honors. He was a soldier whose only concern was the welfare and security of his country. And in that, he was always consistent—on television, in par-

liament, on the streets. I remember once when journalists followed him as he walked past a long line of angry
settlers who were protesting against his peace policy.
One radio reporter asked him:

"Mr. Rabin, don't you want to talk to them?"

"It doesn't interest me," he said. "Forget about them."
He knew where they stood.

I wish I were more like him, I wish I were less sensitive to criticism. When he and I talked, I would disguise
my reactions to gossip. I would say: "You know, Saba,
So-and-so says that I am a snob. Now that's ridiculous."

"Ridiculous," he would reply.

But it still annoyed me to be known as "Rabin's granddaughter." I was proud to be Saba's granddaughter, but I
did not want to share our family life with the public: there
are some things you can talk about with friends, other
things you only discuss at home. Yet for people who did
not know me, I continued to be Rabin's granddaughter,
and in their view, I continued to be open to public scrutiny.

There was one occasion, though, when the tables were
turned. I was fourteen and had gone to stay with some
friends of my grandparents in Massachusetts. I arrived
before my grandparents and had already met some
locals. Then, when Saba showed up, he was introduced
as "Noa's grandfather." He found this amusing, of
course. I told him that now he would know what it was
like to be "Rabin's granddaughter" all the time.

In high school, there was one girl who would always point at me and whisper to her friends when I passed. One day I walked by and she did not react, so I turned back and spoke to her.

"Hey, you forgot to point at me today," I told her.

I suspect Grandpa would not have approved. He would have told me to ignore her, even at the risk of being called a snob. That, at least, was his way of handling things.

I remember one night in September 1995 when the Knesset was debating the second stage of the peace process into the early hours of the morning. Everyone there was agitated, shouting, arguing, throwing insults in all directions. For those of us watching on television, it looked like a circus.

Earlier that evening, a right-wing rally in Zion Square to protest the peace process was attended by some legislators of the opposition parties, including members of the Likud party. Demonstrators chanting inflammatory slogans held up banners saying, "Rabin Is a Traitor," and posters showing Saba dressed in the uniform of an SS officer.

Shevach Weiss, the speaker of the Knesset, felt this should not pass unnoticed and decided that parliament should adopt a resolution condemning incitement to hatred. But before this could happen, he had to give the Likud leader, Benjamin ("Bibi") Netanyahu, a chance to defend his party's position. Netanyahu, who a few hours earlier had watched the rally from a balcony in Zion Square, took the floor.

While he was talking, Grandpa slowly rose and walked out of the chamber. The television cameras followed him as he calmly smoked a cigarette in an outside hall. When the speech was over, he crushed his cigarette and returned to the chamber. But he refused to take his seat. Instead, he spoke into the microphone on the floor of the Knesset.

"Can I speak now?" he asked the speaker softly. "I don't want to take the podium. Here is fine."

He then turned to Netanyahu and said firmly:

"Enough of lies! Let's play the game openly, with our cards on the table. Let's stop tearing this country apart in the name of some artificial unity. Enough of that! Enough of hypocrites."

Only then did he sit down. Jonathan and I, watching on television, wanted to applaud. He was so majestic.

I do not remember the exact sequence of the events that night, but by the time the debate ended, it was three or four o'clock in the morning. I know that at one point Shimon Peres also spoke, and he was brilliant in the way he mocked the right wing. Jonathan and I laughed so loudly that we woke our parents. It was also wonderful to see Peres jumping to the defense of his old Labor Party rival, Saba.

Today, I am still known as "Rabin's granddaughter," but I no longer mind. The lines between Grandpa and Prime Minister have blurred. The Saba that I knew at home was the same man who gave his life for peace. I loved him, admired him, held on to him because he was my grandfather. But now I understand that, if I miss him terribly, it is also because he was my Prime Minister, my protector, the man who made it possible for my entire generation to look to the future with hope.

VIII

Taking Up Arms for Peace

I QUICKLY grew used to the idea of peace. What was strange, though, was that I began to take it for granted when it was still far from assured. My head kept warning me of the obstacles that lay ahead, and there were frequent moments of crisis to remind me that my head was right. But my heart was stronger: I desperately wanted to live in a different Israel, an Israel that was "normal."

Grandpa's will was constantly being tested. In June 1994, in reprisal for provocations, the Israeli air force bombed a military base run by the pro-Iranian Hezbollah movement in the Bekaa valley of southern Lebanon. It provoked all sorts of international protests, but it was also a way of sending a message to Damascus. And it worked. Syria, which had the last word on Arab military activity in Lebanon, responded by tightening its control over Hezbollah.

The following month, on July 18, twenty-six people were killed when a bomb destroyed a building housing the Jewish Assistance Fund in Buenos Aires, home to a large Jewish community. And on July 27, another bomb exploded outside the offices of the United Jewish Appeal in the London borough of Kensington, just in front of the Israeli embassy. Both bombs were blamed on pro-Iranian terrorists opposed to the peace process.

Negotiations with the PLO were continuing, but both the extreme right in Israel and the Palestinian extremist movement, Hamas, were doing what they could to complicate them. The dove of peace had managed to take off, but it was being fired on from all sides.

Grandpa was working around the clock and traveling to the point of exhaustion. I remember that on one occasion, when he seemed ready to drop, he was given a sedative and then slept for fourteen hours without interruption. This prompted some newspapers and Likud politicians to say he had collapsed. His opponents claimed that he was too weak and too old to govern. They reminded the public that during the 1967 war he had also suffered from exhaustion. They said that history was now repeating itself. But he had not collapsed. He was older, but he was also more determined than ever. He had simply followed the orders of his doctor and caught up on his sleep.

The peace process kept moving. On July 25, 1994, Grandpa was in Washington to sign a new peace declaration, this time with Jordan. The two sides committed themselves to opening their borders, establishing direct telephone links, connecting their electricity grids, promoting cooperation between their police forces, and seeking new economic ties. The key point, though, was that the agreement ended forty-six years of hostilities between the neighbors.

This accord occasioned a more relaxed event than the signing with Arafat had. Grandpa with his thick glasses and King Hussein with his white beard smiled warmly at each other, resembling two patriarchs, each happy to forget past offenses, both ready to do what the world expected of them.

Two weeks later, Grandpa paid the first official visit by an Israeli leader to Jordan, meeting King Hussein in his seaside summer palace in Aqaba. It seemed amazing that they were getting on so well, until Saba disclosed to reporters that they had known each other for twenty years. There had always been rumors of secret meetings between them, but now they could at last be confirmed.

On October 26, 1994, the day before Jonathan's twentieth birthday, King Hussein was received in Israel. This time, the two sides signed a peace treaty implementing the Washington Declaration. As a measure of the importance of the occasion, President Clinton and his wife attended along with a dozen foreign ministers, diplomats, businessmen and religious leaders, both Jewish and Muslim. The ceremony took place at the Arava

Crossing, a new border post between Aqaba and Eilat, which only a few days earlier was still blocked by mines. It was exciting to see the first road signs reading: "To Jordan."

Grandpa invited me along to witness my first peace signing. The crossing was decorated with balloons and flags and the mood was cheerful. Young Israeli and Jordanian children welcomed the dignitaries by waving flags. It was fiercely hot when the ceremony took place, at one p.m. Israeli authorities had provided plastic bottles of water, which, once empty, were picked up by the wind and scattered over the desert. Grandpa broke protocol and, to shade himself, put on a white baseball hat, which did not exactly match his dark suit.

I sat on the official platform with the rest of my family, some way from Grandpa, King Hussein and the other V.I.P.'s. (I probably could have seen all of them better on television and I certainly would have been spared the heat.) I was very moved by Saba's speech. I can remember parts of it by heart:

"Good morning, Jordanian mother. Good morning to you, Israeli mother. Today is not like any other. Today is a day of peace and you are bringing your child into a world of peace. . . . The time has now come not only to dream of a better future but to realize it."

King Hussein also recognized that we were living a moment of history:

"This is peace with dignity. This is peace with commitment. This is our gift to peoples and generations to come."

DESPITE the hostility of many Arab countries, despite the Hamas terrorist bombs and the anti-government protests by the Israeli settlers on the West Bank, the steady progress toward peace kept up our spirits.

There was even a fashion show organized in the name of peace. Why not? Peace meant more tourists, more foreign investment, more business activity. And if there are fashion shows in Paris and New York, why not in Israel?

Grandpa was invited to attend a show in Caesarea, forty-five minutes north of Tel Aviv, in the summer of 1995. Because Grandma and Mom were away, he asked me to accompany him. I was delighted. It amused me to think that, for one evening, I would be part of the "in" crowd. Before the show started, Grandpa was invited to say a few words. He naturally spoke about peace, but he also told the audience that he was accompanied by his granddaughter, who probably knew more about fashion than he did. He was relaxed, clearly enjoying the parade of models. But, indeed, he had little idea about women's fashion and kept bombarding me with questions.

"Who's the designer?"

"Jean-Paul Gaultier. . . ."

"Mmm. . . . His clothes are quite unusual . . . do women really wear them?"

I explained that the haute-couture dresses seen in fashion shows are not worn by women on the street, but he remained puzzled.

"I hope my granddaughter won't be seen wearing them," he whispered with a laugh.

Some months later, in September, to celebrate Rosh Hashanah, the Jewish New Year, I wore a long black dress that was rather daring, the see-through material revealing my shoulders and my stomach and, in particular, the ring with which I had pierced my belly button once I graduated from high school. Saba looked at it with an amused but slightly disapproving eye.

"I'd like to meet the designer who made this dress for you," he said ambiguously. "I really would."

Once again, I was reminded: it was not just Noa who was looking provocative; it was also the Prime Minister's granddaughter.

I always felt that I had my family's support in everything I did. But if my grandparents and parents thought I was great, I was aware that I could do better. That was one lesson Saba had taught me: above all, be honest with yourself.

It was certainly no secret at home that I was a bit disorganized, distracted, even clumsy. Whenever I went into the kitchen, Grandma or Mom would ask:

"Noa, don't you have anything to do in your room? Or in the sitting room, perhaps?"

About the only thing that I could cook was pancakes. And even then I left a trail of chaos in the kitchen. I was always envious of my friend Sharon, because she was so meticulous about everything she did. Still, there was hope. Jonathan had always been messy, but he had changed his ways when he joined the army.

As the date of my call-up for military service approached, I decided that I wanted to work for the army radio station. Under military rules, conscripts can apply to be attached to a particular section, though there is no guarantee they will be accepted. Sometimes the army concludes that a given soldier is needed elsewhere. In my case, the army radio station became almost an obsession. I thought of nothing else and prepared myself carefully for the qualifying five-hour written exam and the two interviews that would follow. I knew there was a great deal of competition—it is renowned for being one of the most coveted sections in the army, as it is considered to pave the way for a future career in communications.

I already knew that if I was accepted, there was bound to be some people who would dismiss my achievement on the grounds of nepotism. Wherever I would go and whatever I would do in the army, there would be people who would put my success down to the fact that my grandfather was not only Prime Minister, but also the former chief of staff. I decided not to worry about this in advance and instead concentrated on applying for the job that I would really like.

Once the long application process was over, I just had to be patient. But when the army's letter turning down my application arrived at home, for two days no one dared mention it to me. Then Mom broke the news.

"Noa, they haven't accepted you at the radio station."

I was heartbroken. I had done my best, but that was obviously not enough. I had pinned my hopes on that job and I had failed to get it. For days, I walked around sulking and frowning. Finally, Grandpa brought up the subject and found a way of rebuilding my confidence.

"Noa, it's not the end of the world," he said in a soft voice. "Things will work out for you. If you didn't succeed this time, too bad. You'll find something else, you'll see."

I realized that I had overreacted. I also realized that I was angry and upset largely because my pride had been bruised. And, happily, when I later applied to work for the army newspaper, *Ba'ma'chane,* I was accepted.

I turned eighteen in March 1995, but I did not have much time to dwell on this passage, as I was concentrating on my final school exams in drama. I was directing and acting in a play by Bill Russell called *The Angel's Parade,* about AIDS victims. In a cast of ten, I played two roles: a nurse who had been infected with the AIDS virus while caring for a patient, and a woman who had a truly terrible life. This character had been abused by her father, had been married three times, had become a drug addict, and had gotten pregnant. Only after the birth of the child did she discover that both she and the child were HIV-positive. These were draining and eye-opening roles for me.

We gave four evening performances and my whole family came, except for Grandpa. I had decided to spare him the ordeal that year. The previous year, when he had come to the school play, not only had he sweltered in the heat but he had also been stuck in the audience when he was needed in his office to deal with urgent problems. To compensate for his absence, Grandma attended every performance of our 1995 "season."

I graduated from the Ha'rishonim High School in June 1995 and then spent a month traveling around Europe with Sharon and two other friends, Romi and Nama. Our first port of call was London. It was exciting to be away from home and I liked the idea of not being part of an official delegation. I felt both anonymous and free. At the beginning, we were very active tourists, going to the Tate Gallery, the Barbican Center and the National Gallery. But then our enthusiasm for art waned, the tempo slowed down, and instead of educating ourselves, we meandered through Hampstead and Camden Town and explored Kensington High Street, discovering a good many of the city's McDonald's and ice cream parlors.

From London, we went to Amsterdam, where I was struck by the huge numbers of young people congregating in cafés. We could almost forget that there were any problems in the world. Our last stop was Paris, where we arrived nearly broke. We stayed in a no-star hotel on rue Lafayette and spent our time wandering the narrow streets of the Left Bank and window-shopping. Romi also kept dragging us into supermarkets. She adored studying the shelves of these stores to see what local people had in their fridges. I could never understand this fascination; with the growth of imports in the past few years in Israel, there were few novelties for us to find in Paris supermarkets.

Soon after I returned to Israel, I joined the army. At seven-thirty a.m. on August 15, my family and friends saw me off at Bakum, the call-up base, to start my two and a half weeks of basic training. I had not slept well and managed to arrive ten minutes late. For years, at school and from Grandpa and Jonathan, I had heard about army life. Now it was different. My mother had tears in her eyes. I remember thinking: Can it really be my turn already? I still feel like a kid.

AT FIRST, no one recognized me, but some of the girls knew I was in the group.

"Where is the little idiot who is Rabin's granddaughter?" I heard one ask loudly.

Soon word got around.

"You know who she is?" I heard girls whispering around me.

We boarded a bus and were driven to our training camp, Machane 80. Along the way, I thought about my friends. I knew what they would be doing now that they had waved me on my way: they would be enjoying coffee and croissants at some nearby café and talking about when their turn would come. That is what I had done when my brother and friends had begun military service. But now I was in the bus, with seventeen months of army life ahead of me.

My very first military act was to line up to have my fingerprints taken and be vaccinated against assorted diseases. The next step involved a change of skin when I swapped my civilian clothes for a khaki uniform. In no time, we were all the same. Cultural, physical and economic differences had disappeared. We were all in the same uniform and we all had the same lowly rank. We had all been given a number, which was more important to the army than our names. I felt my past, even my identity, slowly fading away. I had become just another soldier.

Most young Israelis of good health are expected to serve in the army. Israeli Arabs, however, are excluded, because they may well have relatives living in Jordan, Lebanon or Syria, where conflict often erupts. It is natural to wonder if, in battle, they would be ready to fire on their brothers, cousins or friends. Ultra-Orthodox Jews ask to be excluded from military service, arguing that they are prohibited from doing anything on the Sabbath. And our army has to be alert, even on the Sabbath.

Those of us who join the army know that war can break out from one day to another. But military service involves more than defending the nation. Thanks to the army, we are plucked out of our own little worlds and exposed to the full complexity of this land, its European and Middle Eastern features, its religious and secular components, its different economic strata, even its geography. It also prepares us for adulthood, for further studies, for the jobs that will follow.

But the first thing we learn is to obey. On our very first day of training, the girl who was shouting orders was only six months older than I. My first reaction was one of indignation. But I quickly adjusted to her seniority. I shared a room with eight other girls. We had six showers for eighty-four soldiers, so we would line up awaiting our turn with a towel in our hands. And of course everything was done by the clock. We had a schedule for getting up, for showering, for eating, for cleaning up, for telephoning home, for smoking, for going to bed. In the morning, it was a terrible scramble for me: just half an hour to wash, to dress, to put in my contact lenses, to be ready for inspection. The evenings were a little better: we had an hour in which to write letters, smoke and chat before lights-out.

For small violations of discipline, such as chewing gum in front of an officer, eating outside the canteen or falling asleep during classes, the punishment usually involves losing two or three hours of leave time. For anything serious, such as being found with drugs or going absent without leave or committing gross insubordination or firing a weapon without permission, the punishment is imprisonment.

I had no trouble obeying orders, but occasionally I could not resist questioning the rules:

"Why can't I laugh?"

"Because what you're being told is serious."

"Why can't I smoke now?"

"Because it upsets those around you."

I suppose I should have been thinking about issues of national security and earlier generations of soldiers who had built the nation out of sand and ruins, or had lost their lives. Instead, I found myself concentrating on the enormous personal change that I was undergoing.

We had two uniforms—uniform A to wear outside the camp, uniform B to be used during the basic training. They belong to the army and are recycled until they fall to pieces. Fashion is not a major consideration in the ranks. My uniform B was far too large, the sleeves of the shirt hanging over my hands. Sometimes, I thought I would melt, for the temperature reached ninety degrees that summer and the uniform was stifling.

I remember the first few meals we had. Everything smelled the same, everything looked yellow. The meat, the fish, the vegetables—they all looked yellow. I figured this would be the most effective diet of my life. But after a few days, my hunger got the better of me. We were given a set time to eat, and I found myself gulping down the food, eyeing the clock as I went. I cannot deny that, more than once, I asked myself: What am I doing here?

We learned how to use a rifle, even if we were not being sent to the front. I confess that I was not a very good shot. Having been through a series of training sessions with blank ammunition, I was once given target practice with real bullets. I did not exactly drill the bull's-eye with holes.

The general education the army gives is a vital part of the training. It organizes visits to Jerusalem to remind soldiers of its importance. We study our geography and our economic resources and we are taught—if we need to be—to love Israel above all else. Obedience, order, discipline and security are all principles that we are urged to make our own. It is made clear to us that every soldier's personal destiny is linked to Israel's broader destiny. By the time conscripts have finished their basic training, they are supposed to be left in no doubt as to why they are there.

. . .

Taking Up Arms for Peace

ON MY first weekend leave, I felt a bit like a prisoner being released from jail on parole. I jumped into old jeans, gobbled up chocolate and burgers around the clock, stayed up late to see friends, and telephoned everyone I knew to tell them about my new life.

Grandpa wanted to know everything I was doing in the army. He would ask me about the discipline, the food, the working hours, everything. He was very amused to know that I had learned to dress myself in five minutes. And I know that it moved him to see his Noale in uniform, dressed in the same khaki that he wore when he entered Old Jerusalem beside Moshe Dayan after the Six-Day War.

Grandma asked me what I liked least about being a soldier.

"Getting up so early and eating that dreadful yellow food," I replied.

I had no real reason to complain. Apart from the food and the short nights, I did not like having to wear hand-me-down army socks, and I hated polishing my heavy black boots. But I knew that these small hardships paled into insignificance in comparison with the harder times earlier generations had faced. Grandma, a volunteer, was caught up in a war. And when my mother did her military service, conditions were much tougher, with longer training periods and even stricter discipline.

Once the basic training was over, I was lucky not to have to worry about my immediate future. My application to the army newspaper had already been accepted, so I knew not only where I was going, but also that the work was likely to be interesting. The army, of course, has many needs that go beyond the strictly military corps. It looks for people who can type, who can operate a telephone exchange, who can drive, who have experience with computers, who can launder and sew, who can repair things, and so on. Almost everyone seemed to dread being assigned to the military police. Few people wanted to be spying on others.

When I hear about how repetitive and uninspiring are the tasks that some of my girlfriends are required to do, I am reminded how fortunate I am to have a job that I find challenging and consuming. As in any newspaper, each issue focuses on new and different stories. Sometimes my job is to do research on a story for another reporter, which can involve anything from hunting down an interviewee to sifting through archives in search of relevant material for the article.

Occasionally, I do the reporting myself. My first assignment as a cub reporter was to visit a camp where girls were undergoing basic training. I remember arriving at the base at the crack of dawn, somewhat bleary-eyed, armed with questions and accompanied by a photographer. But I was quickly put on my toes, watching the young female commander bark out orders at the girls. And, as my interviews got underway, I was struck by the extent to which the girls I met understood the purpose of what they were doing there.

"Why do you think you need to know how to use a gun?" I asked one.

"Because we are girls, we won't be sent to the front. But some of us may find ourselves in difficult situations, and we must all be prepared."

I AM aware that a role like mine, on the army newspaper, is minor. I have long hours and seem to spend many of them running around. No one would even try to argue that providing news, primarily for distribution within the army itself, is as important as military exercises. Yet, while I know how small my contribution to the army is, I find myself wanting to commit myself fully to the task at hand.

Because when I stop to catch my breath and reflect on the more general implications of being a soldier, I see my military service as a way of giving a part of myself to my country. I feel I am now playing a bit part in the great drama that is Israel's history. In the past the army had to be strong enough to fight and win wars. Today it has to be strong enough for peace. And as the peace process progresses, I am proud to belong to an army that feels strong enough to accept peace.

IX

The Assassin's Shadow

ON DECEMBER 19, 1995, six weeks after Grandpa's death, an amateur video that captured the moment he was gunned down was released to the media. It was the only visual document of his death. That evening, Israeli television planned to show the tape.

My decision to watch it was not difficult, since my Grandpa was involved. If so many other people could watch it, how could I not? I did not think about the pain I might feel at having to witness that terrible moment. The crime had already been committed. The real pain was the loss of Saba.

That morning, the newspaper *Yediot Aharonot* had published exclusive photographs taken from the tape, while Israel's Channel 2 had bought the rights to broadcast it. All copies of that day's edition of the newspaper were quickly snapped up. I bought one, but the photographs of the assassination were of such poor quality, dark and seemingly out of focus, that I could hardly make anything out. I could almost have believed that Neil Armstrong's first steps on the moon were being shown.

That day, Mom and Savta were in Paris to attend a memorial ceremony for Grandpa. Since the end of the traditional Jewish thirty-day mourning period, they had traveled extensively—to Rome to visit with the Pope, to New York, to Washington. Neither of them wanted to see the tape. Jonathan was on duty that evening at the restaurant where he had been working to earn pocket money since he left the military just weeks earlier. Avi, who had already seen the film with Uncle Yuval, was working late at the office and had urged me not to turn on the television. Karin had to stay at her own home. So I was alone at our house in Herzelia.

That evening, after a day's work at the army newspaper, I prepared to watch the tape. Friends had also tried to convince me not to put myself through it, arguing that it would be a harrowing experience that would only add to my sorrow. That afternoon, a journalist had left a message for me asking whether I intended to watch the tape. I refused to answer the call. I knew that Grandpa's death now belonged to the world. These images, like those of the murder of President Kennedy, would soon become part of the archives of history. But for me, it was still a private affair.

I went to my parents' bedroom and, following the news presenters' advice, I switched off the lights and turned up the sound. Along with the rest of Israel, I braced myself to watch Saba's death. The colors, the songs and the music of the peace rally were not shown. Israel's shock and grief in the days and weeks after the assassination were also not recorded. This was only about the crime. Nothing else.

Here is Shimon Peres, people around him. He is led to his car and driven away. Then here comes Saba. He goes down the stairs. Walks to the car. Gets shot. Turns his back. Gets shot again. Collapses. Black picture. The car pulls away. The excerpt was shown in slow motion, then at regular speed, then again in slow motion.

After the first few seconds, the shock hit me. Here he is living. Here he is dead. In a flash, he tumbles to the ground, never to recover.

I started to cry. Even though the pictures were foggy, I could clearly see that it was my Grandpa. I could see the spark of the bullets that hurt him.

Strangely, during the minutes before the assassination, the cameraman had focused on the assassin, a lone figure wearing jeans and a light-colored T-shirt, his arms hanging loosely by his sides. At one moment, policemen seemed to be chatting with him. The tape kept running. It was as if the amateur cameraman suspected the killer's intentions, as if he somehow suspected that what was to happen was a possibility. But the police did not.

Inevitably, the videotape fueled the debate in Israel about why security that evening had been so lax. We later learned that if the parking area had been sealed off, as it should have been, the assassin could not have come close to Grandpa. Newspapers also reported that the killer had planned the assassination on three previous occasions but had been unable to carry it out. Photographs taken that evening showed that he had even removed his yarmulke in order not to stand out in the crowd.

This and more emerged in the aftermath of the murder, along with a host of conspiracy theories about the security failure. But I do not want to be a party to this speculation. Grandpa's bodyguards had protected him steadfastly and loyally for years. In the euphoric atmosphere of the square that night, I suspect they let down their guard. I don't blame them. It just happened that way, and I refuse to keep torturing myself by reliving that scene.

I HAVE often been asked what I think of the assassin. The question has made me reflect a great deal. I am influenced by my desire not to focus on the individual who killed Grandpa and by my unwillingness to blame everyone who was opposed to the peace process. I do not want to say that the entire right wing in Israel is extremist and fanatical, but when I think about the assassin, I cannot ignore the climate that made the murder possible.

Certainly a majority of people on the right did not support Saba's peace policies and would have voted his government out of office if given the chance. But these people are democrats who believe in using legitimate means to change a government. The world of Saba's assassin is quite different. It does not represent the mainstream right. It is an extremist faction that showed it was willing to resort to political murder as a means of changing policy.

Some people abroad may have been surprised by the emergence of this movement. They may have thought that Israelis and Jews were a monolithic bloc, loyal to each other if nothing else. We knew differently. We had seen the extremists in action, we had heard their threats, we knew of their hatred. But we did not know how far they would go.

IN THE last months of Grandpa's life, attacks on him and his policies had grown steadily harsher. I was shocked to see the hate in the eyes of the extremists, to hear them chanting, "Rabin is a murderer, Rabin is a traitor." I hated driving around the country and seeing cars covered with stickers denouncing Saba's policies and insulting him personally. I feared something might happen to him, but I never imagined that the worst possible scenario would become reality.

I saw boys and girls my age, brainwashed by the extremists, parade before the cameras holding posters that showed Grandpa surrounded by skulls and crossbones. I saw men with hoods over their heads burning effigies of Grandpa; sometimes he was portrayed wearing a Palestinian scarf; at other times he was shown wearing the Iron Cross of a Nazi officer.

One television image in particular horrified me. A young man, a Bible in one hand, a revolver in the other, was screaming hatred and the threat of death at Grandpa. I tried not to react, I tried to separate Saba from the person who was being threatened and insulted. I told myself: Noa, don't worry. They don't know Saba as you do. They don't know how strong, how determined, how honest he is.

I never told Saba how much I worried about him. When I talked to him, my fears would vanish. He was at peace with himself and with what he was doing. The demonstrations did not turn him away from his chosen path. He did not even seem to mind being called a murderer, as long as he was doing what he believed in.

"It's better to ignore them," he would say. And I would feel reassured.

I know that all this abuse upset him, but he never reacted openly, not even in the family. He and Grandma had decided that they would defend themselves with humor and irony.

One evening in 1995, there was an angry demonstration outside their apartment building in Ramat Aviv. Grandma arrived home first and was met with cries of "Rabin is a traitor." Then Grandpa was given the same treatment. When he reached their apartment, Grandma joined the chorus:

"Rabin is a traitor. Rabin is a traitor."

He burst out laughing.

"Oh, come on," he said. "I've had enough of that downstairs."

JONATHAN was the first to provide an accurate definition of the assassin, and it was one that I readily adopted. He was just a gun, a robot deprived of any human identity, someone who had been indoctrinated by a well-oiled system of hate, a system that was deeply ingrained in our society.

Like my brother and me, the assassin was brought up in Herzelia, and like Jonathan, he had served in the army. But he was not like us. He attended a religious school and, from an early age, was drawn into a world ruled by extremist rabbis and other fanatical opinion-makers. Their constant incitement to violence reminded me of the methods used by the Nazis and Fascists in their rise to power. They were united by hate. They all carried the gun that killed Saba. Yigal Amir, the assassin, was simply the one who pulled the trigger.

After the killing, some of these groups suddenly sought understanding of, and acceptance for, their views, but they were not ready to accept responsibility for what they had done. They had had no qualms about organizing ugly protests. They had cheerfully launched an evil crusade against Grandpa. They had carried out wild provocations. But then they wouldn't take responsibility for the consequences of their actions. "Victory has a hundred fathers, and defeat is an orphan." In the aftermath of Saba's death, this old saying seems particularly appropriate. The right-wing, so-called "democratic" struggle was a failure. Today, those who incited violence do not want to be held accountable for it. Everyone is trying desperately to wash their hands of blame.

THE ASSASSIN's family received wide media coverage, and this in part spotlighted the home environment in which he was brought up. I blame his family as much as I blame him.

His brother admitted providing the nine-millimeter ammunition which he had previously converted into explosive bullets. He claimed that he did not know how his brother would use the bullets: "He's my brother. I just gave them to him, that's all."

So what were the bullets for? one might ask. In the back garden of their house, police also found grenades, detonators and plastic explosives.

The assassin's mother sent a letter of condolence to Grandma. I read it and was not at all convinced that it echoed genuine feelings. It was not a simple handwritten letter from one woman to another which might have said:

"My name is Geula and I am the mother of two sons . . ."

Instead, it was typewritten and full of commonplace phrases.

Her letter meant nothing to me. Grandpa had been killed by a system, and it was up to the system to show genuine remorse. In my opinion, this letter showed none.

MOURNING is a pure sentiment. I do not wish to stain it with hate. I feel no need for revenge. I want to bury myself in my own memories, my sweet memories of Saba, which will stay with me forever. That is why I try to avoid specific references to the murderer. But I cannot promise that I will always feel this way. It is not easy. Even now, I cannot prevent myself from feeling contempt for the assassin's world.

It made my blood boil to see the murderer in court, looking relaxed, chewing gum, even laughing, evidently still convinced that he had done the right thing. And I could not stomach it when a television station showed the triumphal return home of a young right-wing woman suspected of being an accomplice to the killer. I now understood why Saba called the extremists "ayatollahs." His death proved him right.

As I see it, Israel is like a divided body, healthy on one side, stricken with cancer on the other. And that cancer is the extreme right. It was the cancer that killed Grandpa. It is the cancer that is still trying to kill Israel. How can we rid ourselves of this cancer?

I am not a politician nor a sociologist, but I believe that only through education can we bridge the huge gulf between the religious extremists and the rest of us. Tolerance must be taught in our schools, but also the respect for all opinions and the wisdom of a united Israel. Surely one day these extremists will concede that most of my generation wants to live in peace, and that extremism will never allow that blessed event to take place.

During the days immediately after Saba's death, many people urged my family to call for the unity of Israel at this moment of tragedy. When one important rabbi visited Grandma, he asked her to "calm the nation down." I could not help thinking:

It's up to you to do something. . . . You're the rabbi!

We had already paid a high enough price. Why should we, the victims, be calling for unity? It was now the turn of the religious schools and the right-wing institutions and the rabbis to call for restraint. They had divided the nation; now it was up to them to reunite it.

Today the central question raised by Saba's death is not why there was a security failure at Kings of Israel Square. It is why such a crime could take place in a so-called enlightened country like Israel. This is the reason that we must concentrate on the ills of a society that can produce such monsters as the assassin. His name is Yigal Amir, but so many others could have taken his place. The issue is not Amir the man or the Amirs as a family, but the system that made the killing possible. The writing was on the wall, but we did not see it until Saba's death. Now it is no longer possible to ignore it.

One night after my grandfather's murder, Grandma and I had a long talk. I told her that my only consolation was that Saba died unaware that such a thing could have happened to him, that he died without knowing that he had been killed by a Jewish criminal, by "one of us," as we would say. Savta disagreed. Had Saba been aware of the danger, she said, his death could have been averted. But I could not help thinking: If Saba had to die in this way, it was better for him to know nothing about those who did it.

X

November 6, 1995

AT SIX-THIRTY on the morning of Grandpa's funeral, I sat at his desk, took a sheet of paper with his personal letterhead, and began to write what would be my last letter to him.

Shimon Sheves, one of Saba's closest friends, was the first to suggest that I speak at the funeral as the representative of the family. I hesitated. But my family convinced me to do it.

The night before, I had tried to write what I would say. I left my grandparents' apartment in Ramat Aviv and went to Herzelia in search of some peace. But even at home, I could not find the right inspiration. The phone kept ringing, there was a mass of unopened telegrams, and I felt in a daze. I was simply unable to tie one word to the next. I had the letter in my head, but the sentences would not take shape. I returned to Ramat Aviv, leaving papers scattered across my bedroom. I told my mother that I might have to improvise.

It had been a strange and dark day, the first day without Saba. When Grandma awoke that morning, she said out of the blue: "Something terrible happened last night, didn't it?" She was thinking of my mother, who had been ill. Then she saw my mother.

"But . . . Dalia is here . . . and Abale?"

I was still fast asleep and only later did Mom tell me of my grandmother's painful return to reality. By the time I opened my eyes, both of them had been up for hours. For a moment, I too was confused. I did not know why I was in their bed. I enjoyed a few seconds of grace before remembering. Then the nightmare returned.

I rose without rising. I walked without walking. People arrived and left. There must have been newspapers on the table. I probably glanced at them. People must have spoken of the assassin, but I was somewhere else. A deep sorrow, the first of my life, was to take hold of me for a week.

Around midday, we set off for Jerusalem to pay our last respects to Saba, in a ceremony called Haskava. Saba's coffin had already left from the hospital in a command car. Our little convoy drove slowly, passing crowds of men and women, young and old. I could not see their faces, but I was impressed by the mass they formed. As I looked up toward the blue sky, I caught sight of billboards. The advertisements had been ripped down overnight and replaced with messages of mourning set against black backgrounds. One sign bore the words of

Shlomo Artsi's popular song, "Where are there people like that man? . . ." Tears rolled down my face. There was no other person like him. And for me, there never will be.

At the Knesset, ministers, members of Parliament and other public figures walked slowly past the coffin that was placed in front of the building, and then came to shake our hands. It seemed unreal to think that this simple coffin draped in the blue-and-white Israeli flag contained my grandfather. Suddenly his life and all his deeds were compressed into a wooden box. I felt offended, offended for him. He should not be lying there in a box. He belonged here, where we needed him, where he wanted to be.

I cannot remember how long the Haskava ceremony lasted, but I recall that Uncle Yuval recited Kaddish, the prayer for the dead, in memory of Grandpa. I admired my uncle's ability to speak at such a difficult moment, when I could hardly say a word. Even a single short prayer like Kaddish would have been too much for me. I began to wonder if I could speak in public the following day at the funeral. But Uncle Yuval was an example to me.

When we returned to Ramat Aviv, the apartment soon filled again with visitors. And it was then that I went home to try to write my letter to Grandpa. I returned around midnight, empty-handed. Everyone had left and we three women went to bed, drained.

Shortly before six-thirty a.m., Mom woke me and suggested that I try to write again. It might be easier in the morning, she said. And she was right. Now the words flowed easily, naturally, as if Saba were seated in front of me, smiling, encouraging me. He seemed so close. I knew he was dead, yet I still could not believe it. I could feel his warmth, his strength, filling the room. And I was in his chair.

My conversation with him was so real, my feelings were so intense, that I wrote my message to him in just a few minutes.

I asked Mom and Savta to read my draft. Aunt Rachel also read it. When I read it to Jonathan, I burst into tears. I was worried that I would cry at the funeral, but my family was very supportive. I remember reminding myself repeatedly:

The most important thing is to say everything, to speak clearly, to get to the end of the speech, to tell him everything I want to say, to make him hear me.

I tried to be inspired by Saba's own strength.

We set off from Tel Aviv around eleven a.m. to return to the Knesset in Jerusalem. Saba was still waiting where we had left him the day before. He had not been alone for a single moment. Thousands of people had passed in front of him, lighting remembrance candles or leaving little written messages. The road to the Knesset and Knesset Square itself were bulging with thousands more people. They, just like me, could not believe he was dead. It was as if seeing the coffin was the only way they could be convinced that the nightmare was real.

When we reached Jerusalem, Grandma, Mom and Uncle Yuval were taken to the Prime Minister's official home in Jerusalem for a private meeting with King Hussein. The rest of us—family and close aides of Grandpa—were led to the Prime Minister's office in the Knesset. It is a rather formal office. On the door, it said simply: "Yitzhak Rabin, Prime Minister and Defense Minister." Saba, who normally worked at a nearby office in the Prime Minister's building, used this room when he attended the Knesset. I had visited him there only once, on the night the Knesset swore in the new government in 1992. A memory flashed across my mind. We had arrived at his office and he called out:

"Leah . . ."

And she replied with a laugh:

"Yes, Mr. Prime Minister." She said it with a mock air, imitating a line from "Yes, Minister," a satirical British television comedy series that they loved to watch together.

Now the Prime Minister's chair in the Knesset office was empty. We waited there for about half an hour before being led to the Knesset speaker's office. President Clinton and his wife arrived, accompanied by President Weizman. At one point, President Clinton spoke to me. Although I cannot recall our conversation, I do remember feeling touched that he admired Grandpa so much.

The idea of Saba as a historic figure did not crystallize for me until after his funeral. (I think Jonathan had long been aware of Saba's greatness.) It was then that I understood that the whole world had come to pay their last respects to him, not because of the way he had died, but because of the way he had lived. During the ceremony, however, I could think only about his absence. With so many important people around, the gathering reminded me of the several peace ceremonies of the previous two years in which Saba and Shimon Peres had participated. The only difference was that Saba was no longer there.

We left the office around one p.m. and went to stand near the coffin, where we were soon joined by Grandma, Mom and Uncle Yuval. Dignitaries were arriving from all over the world. They stood silently before the closed coffin and then expressed their condolences to Grandma and other family members. There were so many people around us, yet I could feel only emptiness.

We watched the coffin being lifted and carried out of the Knesset by six army generals and two police commanders. It was then put on a military vehicle. Thousands of eyes were looking at us, cameras were flashing constantly, journalists were everywhere. There were lines of black cars, dozens of security agents and a huge crowd of mourners. I tried to close myself off from my surroundings, to be alone with my own grief.

The cortege behind Saba's coffin set off slowly for Mount Herzl. Endless lines of people on the sides of the road accompanied Saba on his last journey. They seemed to form a canyon of sadness that led all the way to his final resting place. Grandpa's Jerusalem had become the capital of the world. Now Saba was lying at the heart of this eternal city, and the world's eyes were on his coffin.

Finally, we took our seats in the front row of the mourners. It was hot, with only a few clouds smudging a clear blue sky. Sirens sounded for two minutes, echoing over the pines and cedars of Mount Herzl. When the sirens stopped, the silence grew so profound that it was almost painful.

Grandma and Mom were to my right. Jonathan was to my left, in military uniform. One month later, he would be released from the army, but he had made a point of wearing his uniform in honor of Saba, who was so proud of him as a soldier.

Around us sat an entire United Nations of important dignitaries—President Clinton, King Hussein, President Mubarak, the Queen of the Netherlands, Prime Minister Major of Britain, the German President and Prime Minister, the Prime Minister of Russia, the Secretary-General of the United Nations, Boutros Boutros-Ghali. . . . Grandpa's family was not alone.

Finally, the ceremony began, with Uncle Yuval reciting Kaddish, as he had done in the Knesset the previous day.

"Magnified and sanctified be his great Name in the world which he hath created according to his will. May he establish his kingdom in your lifetime and in your days, and in the lifetime of all the house of Israel, speedily and at a near time; and say ye, Amen.

"Let his great Name be blessed for ever and ever.

"Blessed, praised and glorified, exalted, extolled and honored, adored and lauded, be the name of the Holy One, blessed be he, beyond all blessings and hymns, praises and songs, which are uttered in the world; and say ye, Amen.

"May there be abundant peace from heaven, and life for us, and for all Israel; say ye, Amen.

"May he who maketh peace in his high places make peace for us and for all Israel; say ye, Amen."

I tried to keep myself upright, awaiting my turn to speak. I did not know when my name would be called. I tried to pay attention to what the other speakers were saying, but it was not easy. People spoke from the heart, out of grief, but their words seemed to roll over me. I cannot pretend that I can remember all the speeches in detail. But later, when I saw them again on television, they seemed familiar, as if they were already stored away in my subconscious.

King Hussein spoke without a prepared text, deeply pained at the loss of his former enemy whom he now called "a brother, a colleague and a friend, a man, a soldier."

He turned to Grandpa's coffin and said:

"You lived as a soldier, you died as a soldier for peace."

He then went on:

"He was a man of courage . . . and he was endowed with one of the greatest virtues that any man can have. He was endowed with humility. . . . He had courage, he had vision and he had a commitment to peace. And standing here I commit myself before you, before my people in Jordan, before the world, to continue to do my utmost to insure that we leave a similar legacy. . . ."

President Clinton spoke of Grandpa as a "partner and friend," even drawing sad smiles when he remembered lending Grandpa a black tie and helping him to straighten it before the gala dinner marking the fiftieth anniversary of the United Nations only two weeks earlier in New York.

"It is a moment I will cherish as long as I live."

But Clinton was also eager to keep alive Grandpa's dream of peace, and he urged Israelis to heed the lessons of the tragedy.

"Your Prime Minister was a martyr for peace, but he was a victim of hate. Surely we must learn from his martyrdom that if people cannot let go of the hatred of their enemies, they risk sowing the seeds of hatred among themselves. I ask you, the people of Israel, on behalf of my nation that knows its own long litany of loss—from Abraham Lincoln to President Kennedy to Martin Luther King—do not let that happen to you."

Shimon Peres remembered that only two days earlier he and Grandpa had joined hands at Kings of Israel Square to sing the "Song of Peace."

"You did not leave us a will," he said, addressing Saba, "but you left us a path which we will follow with determination and faith. The nation is crying. I hope these will be tears for unity, tears for peace among us, and peace with our neighbors."

President Mubarak, on his first trip ever to Israel, spoke more formally, calling Grandpa "a courageous leader and a recognized statesman ... who defied the prejudices of the past to tackle the most complicated of problems."

I also remember hearing Sheves's familiar voice. So often in the past I had heard him in conversation with Saba. Now he spoke again: "Our dear Yitzhak ... You were a loving husband, father and grandfather. ... We worked together for thirty years ... and our paths never once diverged. ... I loved you. ... Go in peace, Mr. Prime Minister; go in peace, Yitzhak Rabin." I withdrew further into myself, taking his words with me.

And after each address, the speaker would walk over to our family to pay his respects to Grandma.

. . .

THEN my name was called out.

Soldiers guided me to the podium. Now it was my turn to fill the immense silence that enveloped Mount Herzl. I dedicated myself to this silence, without paying attention to the audience or the media. I thought only of Saba and my family. I was there, entirely with Grandpa. I hoped that he too was there with me.

I tried to hold back my tears and began reading:

"Please excuse me for not wanting to talk about peace. I want to talk about my grandfather.

"You always awake from a nightmare, but since yesterday I have been continually awakening to a nightmare. It is not possible to get used to the nightmare of life without you. The television never ceases to broadcast pictures of you, and you are so alive that I can almost touch you—but only almost, and I won't be able to anymore.

"Grandfather, you were the pillar of fire in front of the camp and now we are left in the camp alone, in the dark; and we are so cold and so sad.

"I know that people talk in terms of a national tragedy, and of comforting an entire nation, but we feel the huge void that remains in your absence when grandmother doesn't stop crying.

"Few people really knew you. Now they will talk about you for quite some time, but I feel that they really don't know just how great the pain is, how great the tragedy is; something has been destroyed.

"Grandfather, you were and still are our hero. I want you to know that every time I did anything, I saw you in front of me.

"Your appreciation and your love accompanied us every step down the road, and our lives were always shaped by your values. You, who never abandoned anything, are now abandoned. And here you are, my ever-present hero, cold, alone, and I cannot do anything to save you. You are missed so much.

"Others greater than I have already eulogized you, but none of them ever had the pleasure I had to feel the caresses of your arms, your soft hands, to merit your warm embrace that was reserved only for us, to see your half-smile that always told me so much, that same smile which is no longer, frozen in the grave with you.

"I have no feelings of revenge because my pain and feelings of loss are so large, too large. The ground has been swept out from below us, and we are groping now, trying to wander about in this empty void, without any success so far.

"I am not able to finish this; left with no alternative, I say goodbye to you, hero, and ask you to rest in peace, and think about us, and miss us, as down here we love you so very much. I imagine angels are accompanying you now, and I ask them to take care of you because you deserve their protection.

"We will love you, Saba, forever."

I HAD tried so hard to be strong. But in the end, I broke down. And when I rejoined my family, I could not stop sobbing. I did not hear the next speaker, Eitan Haber, Grandpa's speechwriter and close friend. Perhaps that was lucky. It would have been too much for me. Even later, when I heard him on television, I was overwhelmed.

"Yitzhak, this is the final speech," he began. "There will not be another one. For a whole generation, more than thirty-five years, you were my teacher, counselor and leader. You were my father. . . ."

That was indeed the final speech. There will be no more speeches from Saba.

THE MOMENT had come to bury Grandpa in the cemetery on Mount Herzl. Other great figures of Israeli history, such as Golda Meir, had been buried there before him. This is the place where he would rest in peace unto eternity. We had all received something from him, and we were now also burying a part of ourselves with him. A silent crowd gathered around the tomb. A voice whispered in my ear:

"You were the only one who knew how to talk to your grandfather."

I recognized the voice. I looked up and I saw President Clinton.

Grandpa's coffin was slowly lowered into the grave. I kept saying to myself, This is not a coffin, it is a man. The bearers were struggling with the weight and at one point the coffin almost slipped. I felt a deep pain in my stomach, as if a knife were stabbing me.

One by one, mourners came by and, according to the Jewish tradition, shoveled some earth on the coffin. I will never forget that earth, the sound of it striking the coffin. I trembled, I held on to my mother from behind, my head on her shoulder. She held me up, I held her up. Why did we have to live through this horror?

Soldiers presented arms and then fired a three-salvo salute which made me shudder. Saba would stay on Mount Herzl forever. He had been taken from me. Everything was over.

WHEN the whole family returned to Ramat Aviv, we tried to push aside the awfulness of the day by remembering Grandpa differently. Jonathan and I sat together and reminisced about sweet moments we had spent with him.

The following day, we both appeared on Gidi Gov's television talk show and continued to talk about Saba as if he were still alive. How could we use the past tense so soon after his death? We told stories about our Grandpa—not about the Prime Minister—and we laughed a lot. Every memory we had of him made us feel warm. The laughter born of good memories was reassuring.

It was of course not accidental that we appeared on Gov's show. He symbolized the pleasant part of that terrible Saturday just three days earlier. He was among the last people to talk to Saba. He was certainly the most appropriate person to lead us through a conversation about Grandpa that was both joyful and sad. Only with him did we feel free to laugh without feeling it was inappropriate. In truth, there are no rules about mourning. Laughter can sometimes move people even more than sorrow.

On November 12, we returned to Kings of Israel Square. More than five hundred thousand people came to honor Saba in what was now called Yitzhak Rabin Square. I sat on the stage with my family, the same stage where Saba had stood eight days before. A huge portrait of him hung behind us. It was as if he were overseeing the rally, staring out at the sea of candles and tears. Grandma spoke to him in her speech.

"When you died, Israel stopped to catch its breath . . . if you could see, Yitzhak, if I could tell you everything that's been happening in the country this past week, you wouldn't believe me. . . . Thousands of people have been coming from all four corners of the world, Jews, Muslims, Christians . . . can you believe it? Please believe me."

An estimated thirty thousand young people kept a vigil at the square throughout the night, huddling around candles and singing songs of peace. The stone wall near the scene of the crime had turned into a patchwork of tributes, covered with hundreds of messages to Grandpa, poems and drawings. Grandma was right—never before had such a thing happened. Grandpa's modesty and realism would have prevented him from believing that such an outpouring of support was possible, unless he saw it with his own eyes. I hold on to the thought that somewhere he has, and still is, watching, with amazement.

After Saba's death, I received many letters from Israel and all over the world. I am ashamed to admit that I have not answered most of them. I simply lacked the strength to write personal letters and felt that a standard printed reply would satisfy no one. I hope to answer all of them one day. They touched me deeply and made me understand that I was not alone.

It is clear to me that many people around the world saw Grandpa's death as a great political tragedy. I was Rabin's granddaughter and they reached out to me, but I think they also saw me as a child of Israel, a symbol of the peace for which he gave his life.

November 6, 1995

After I read all those letters, I was able to write again, to delve into my memories, to release my emotions, to speak to Saba in print. Writing this book was my way of keeping him alive in my heart. It was also my way of making sure that no one would forget him.

Epilogue

IT WAS not easy to start writing this book. Everything was so fresh, the pain was still so raw. Inside my head, thoughts, ideas, feelings, uncertainties, spun around like broken pieces of mirror, reflecting and distorting, refusing to obey either head or heart. All I could think was, I miss you, Saba, I miss you.

And I kept wondering, do I have anything to say that has not already been said?

Great leaders had spoken eloquently at Grandpa's funeral. I had addressed my last words to him as he lay in his coffin. Newspapers around the world had published lengthy obituaries. Radio and television stations had dedicated endless hours to analyzing his life. Rarely has a man been buried to such a chorus of tributes.

And now the world was moving on. The governments in Washington, London, Paris and everywhere else had other problems to worry about. Israel had a new Prime Minister in Shimon Peres. The peace process seemed to be gathering pace. The PLO had assumed control of more towns on the West Bank. There were even hopes for a settlement with Syria. Then, as the bombs blew up in Israel, we were reminded of how many roadblocks there are on the road to peace. Was there any purpose to looking back when the future still had to be shaped?

But I felt the need to write. I was afraid of becoming used to the sorrow that had grown like a gnarled tree inside me. I did not want to accept Grandpa's death until I had understood his life.

I have always liked writing, and Grandpa never failed to encourage me. During his lifetime he would keep a folder containing the poems I would scribble for him. Now, at his death, I have continued to write for him. I have collected my memories of him and made it into a book. Although I shall look after it, this book is for him.

I admit that there was something selfish about my decision. Writing has helped me to deal with my grief, to overcome my fear of living without him. His death closed a chapter in my life. The bullets that killed him also put an end to my childhood. And now I must face a new reality, of which he is no longer a part.

But I think I can contribute something too. For all that has been written and said about Grandpa, not many people knew him well. It is true that I knew him only as an admiring granddaughter, but I saw him as few others could: as a warm and loving man. When he was alive, I was keen to remain silent about who my grandfather was. Now that he has gone, this book is also my way of sharing him with the world.

I feel I have been on a long personal journey with him, and this has comforted me. But it has also been a voyage in which I have discovered the "other" Grandpa, the statesman, the forger of peace. And having been his little ambassador during his lifetime, I now feel a special responsibility to defend his memory and to promote his ideas.

Above all, I hope my memories of Grandpa will touch young people. I want young Israelis, young Arabs in our neighboring countries, and other young people to know that behind the politician there was a man of honesty and principle, a man who never stopped believing that his dream of Middle East peace could become a reality. I want everyone to know that a politician, this politician, can be a source of inspiration.

I cannot claim to speak for all young Israelis. I recognize that I was brought up in a privileged environment. There was nothing typical about being "Rabin's granddaughter." But I went to government schools, I was raised in a democracy and I became a soldier. And I know with all my heart that most young Israelis want to live in peace.

Can Israelis live at peace with each other? Can we live at peace with our neighbors? When I think that it was pure hatred that murdered Grandpa, my optimism wavers. But then I remember how he might have reacted:

"Noale, nothing is impossible if it is the right thing to do. Failure is just another reason to keep trying. . . ."

Grandpa's death was a high price to pay for his failure to persuade all Israelis that the future could be different. What my family has lost is irreplaceable. And most Israelis have been devastated. But I know he would want us to keep trying.

I have tried to imagine how Saba would react to my book. When I close my eyes, I can see him, sitting at home, wearing a light-colored T-shirt, a newspaper on his knees, a half-smile playing on his lips. He is peering at me through his glasses, with a look of amused curiosity, as if he were asking:

So, Noale, how's your book? Are you giving away all my secrets?

But when I open my eyes, I see a man much larger than any book, a man who left a mark on much more than his granddaughter and his mourning family.

He stood astride this country's history and had the courage and imagination to turn a page. He reached out for the impossible and brought it within reach. And when he died, he left a legacy of hope to Israel, the Middle East and the world.

Epilogue

We must remain vigilant to all the threats against Israel, from within and from outside our country. But we owe it to ourselves to complete the peace process. We also owe it to my grandfather. More than funeral orations or memoirs, peace will be the lasting monument to his life.

May his memory be blessed.

March 1996

Postscript

Israel, February 1997

Dear Saba,

It has been almost a year and a half since that black Sabbath, and today I am looking back at what has happened to us and to me since then. It seems that almost everything has been said about you, about the murder, about the pain and the sea of tears. But I am unable to gauge fully the time that has passed. I still ache and, just like in the aftermath of your death, I find myself wanting to talk to you, to tell you more.

A year and a half, Saba, and nothing seems to be like it was. We try very hard to keep up our old pattern of life—the family—but it's not the same. Every gathering around you was happy, but now we gather around your absence. We are like a jigsaw puzzle with a crucial piece missing. We know that the gap is there. We live with it. But we can never fill it.

When you were alive we went through tough times together, but we always continued to be optimistic, and happy with our lot. Today we are different. And when I try to imagine you looking at me now—it's hard. I'm not the same girl you knew only a year and a half ago.

After you were murdered, I wrote this book about you, and for you. In doing so I hoped that in some way I could share and keep alive the Yitzhak Rabin whom Mickey, Jonathan and I knew as our Saba. When the book was published I took one month's leave from the army newspaper and I traveled across the United States and Europe to talk about you. I spoke about you with a love and a longing that only grew stronger the more I talked.

In your public appearances and dealings with the press you always prided yourself on being honest. Even if it meant not giving people exactly what they wanted to hear, you would not camouflage your feelings for the sake of the "show." I tried to follow your example.

People responded with overwhelming warmth and generosity. Both Jews and non-Jews, from all walks of life, genuinely cared about you. I carried their words of sympathy with me as I moved, admittedly in a daze sometimes, from one country, culture and time zone to another.

But then something started to worry me. Every now and then I would suddenly feel that we were drawing apart, that there was distance growing between you and me. That feeling was unbearable and it sent me into a panic. I began to think: What would make you happy, and what would make you sad? How can I make you proud of me—and what would cause you to be ashamed?

It was then that I decided to give up my work on the army newspaper and apply to become an officer. It was an important step for me because I remembered how much you wanted Jonathan to be an officer. I thought that by becoming one myself, somehow I would keep you by my side a little longer; that in some way, you would be able to protect me in this world which seemed to be so much more precarious and dangerous since the three bullets took you away from it.

On the day of your funeral and during the months that followed, it was as if the world had stopped turning. For once, everyone seemed to be in agreement. "Yitzhak Rabin" became a slogan, almost a synonym for "Peace." Both in Israel and abroad hospitals, public squares, streets and schools were created in your memory, or renamed after you. Mom and Savta were invited throughout the world to accept prizes on your behalf and to participate in rallies in your honor.

But that wasn't all. Your peace policies, which were being kept alive by your successors, were accepted and praised. It was as though no one had ever been called a traitor—least of all you. This surge of goodwill seemed to mark the beginning of a new era. However, hard as

I tried to believe in it, deep inside I knew that this unity was terribly fragile and, alas, only temporary.

In February—less than half a year after your assassination—came a wave of terror in Israel that claimed the lives of innocent bystanders. The perpetrators were preaching indiscriminate murder; their goal was to murder the peace process.

And Saba, you were no longer here to look straight into the eyes of your people to quell their fears and communicate a feeling of calm. You were not here to reassure everyone that there was a leader who not only cared, but who also had the experience and knowledge of how to cope with the crisis. That, at the top, there was someone who could answer the criticism from the right-wing lobbies, someone who could be trusted to find a solution, if not immediately, then at least soon.

The huge void you left behind had become glaringly obvious to us all. It seemed that there was no replacement for you, no one who could command the country like you. Then, on May 29, 1996, came the great blow—Labor's agonizing defeat in the elections. We felt that you had been murdered again, but this time the path toward peace had been killed with you. We had let you down. We felt numb. What next?

To our relief, it was only a matter of time before we learned that even your old opponents had realized that there is no safer road than the one you led us down. The peace agreements over which you labored with such artistry, day and night, were now being signed by another man, with a different name.

So Benjamin Netanyahu agreed to meet Yasir Arafat, Hebron was handed over to Palestinian rule, and the autonomy of the territories on the West Bank became an issue worthy of discussion. One by one, the changes you had foreseen were being implemented—they were taking longer to materialize, but they were nevertheless becoming real.

In hindsight, there is an extraordinary irony about the situation. No playwright could ever have imagined a destiny more tragic than yours. Let me sum up the story: A man of war, dressed in the uniform of peace, is killed by a brother in the last stages of a long-fought battle. The murder is the result of a fierce argument about which is the right road to peace. But in the final act, the victim's opponents, the very men who were supported by the murderer, are seen walking down the same road. Isn't this the stuff Greek tragedies are made of?

But Saba, believe me, this peace is yours. And it's important that you know it—even though you never sought honors and credits. It is yours. And even if the most awful injustice has been done, I find some consolation in the fact that, when all is said and done, you won.

I wonder what you must be thinking as you watch over us. There are times when I hope you don't see what's going on, as it would break your heart. Other times, I hope intensely that you're sharing every moment with us. I still miss you badly, all the time. But I am trying, guided by my memory of your courage and resilience, to be strong.

Missing you,
Noale

WITHOUT the support of my family, this book would not have been possible. I thank them for the encouragement, the advice and the patience that they unfailingly gave me at every stage.

Build Your Library with

SCHOCKEN BOOKS

THE PERIODIC TABLE
by Primo Levi
0-8052-1041-5

LOVE'S WORK
A Reckoning with Life
by Gillian Rose
0-8052-1078-4

THE SCHOCKEN BOOK OF CONTEMPORARY JEWISH FICTION
edited by Ted Solotaroff and Nessa Rapoport
0-8052-1065-2

ALL RIVERS RUN TO THE SEA
Memoirs
by Elie Wiesel
0-8052-1028-8

FRAGMENTS
Memories of a Wartime Childhood
by Binjamin Wilkomirski
0-8052-4139-6

Available at your local bookstore, or call toll-free:
1-800-733-3000 (credit cards only).